SELF-REGULATION and MINDFULNESS ACTIVITIES for

SENSORY PROCESSING DISORDER

SELF-REGULATION and MINDFULNESS ACTIVITIES for

SENSORY PROCESSING DISORDER

Creative Strategies to Help Children Focus and Remain Calm

Stephanie M. Foster PhD, OTR/L, RYT

Illustrations by Irena Freitas

ROCKRIDGE
PRESS

For general information on our other products and services or to obtain technical support, please contact our Customer Care Department within the United States at (866) 744-2665, or outside the United States at (510) 253-0500.

Rockridge Press publishes its books in a variety of electronic and print formats. Some content that appears in print may not be available in electronic books, and vice versa.

TRADEMARKS: Rockridge Press and the Rockridge Press logo are trademarks or registered trademarks of Callisto Media Inc. and/or its affiliates, in the United States and other countries, and may not be used without written permission. All other trademarks are the property of their respective owners. Rockridge Press is not associated with any product or vendor mentioned in this book.

Interior and Cover Designer: Mando Daniel

Art Producer: Tom Hood

Editor: Seth Schwartz

Production Manager: Michael Kay

Production Editor: Andrew Yackira

Illustrations ©2020 Irena Freitas

Author photo courtesy of Leslie Edward

ISBN: Print 978-1-64611-257-9
eBook 978-1-64611-258-6
R0

To my mother, Ellen Bavaro, who very courageously taught me self-regulation from the very beginning.

To the children and families of Kid's Work. Thank you for teaching me self-regulation every day and for trusting me to guide you on your journeys.

Contents

Introduction

For most of us, our lives are a wonderful mix of sensory input and responses. Life is basically a series of events that come in through our sensory systems, are processed in our brains, and then our bodies respond. We make daily adjustments in our activities to maintain a "just right" state. Though we frequently try to improve our sensory regulation, we don't necessarily realize that's what we are doing. Whether we climb into cozy pajamas at the end of a long day or take a walk outside after sitting at a desk for hours at a time, we are attempting to regulate our sensory systems. Children with sensory processing disorder (SPD) have difficulty making adjustments to reach that "just right" state, so they need to learn techniques and strategies to help them navigate everyday life. Whether or not we have SPD, if we are unable to give our body what it needs, we become cranky, inattentive, and unproductive. Living in the moment (that is, practicing mindfulness) helps children with SPD, and all of us really, better understand and attend to our sensory needs so that we can reach a happier, more attentive, and more productive state.

I am honored to be your guide on this journey to help your child. After 30-plus years of practicing as an occupational therapist (OT) both in private practice and school-based settings, my passion is helping families understand their child's sensory needs. My therapeutic philosophy is that understanding parents' and children's sensory processing patterns is key to influencing the family's relationships, self-regulation, and overall happiness. I work with families to help figure out why kids are unable to self-regulate and how to manage meltdowns and other disruptive behaviors. I firmly believe in occupational therapy's non-pharmacological approach to helping children thrive in their true occupations of living, learning, and playing.

This book is divided into two parts. Part one provides you with some background on sensory processing disorder and self-regulation and will touch upon mindfulness and what that means. Whether you are a parent, guardian, primary caregiver, or teacher, you can learn to read your child's cues and respond in a way that's helpful. As you come to understand your child's sensory processing abilities, the meaning behind their behavior will become clearer, and you can help your child become happier and function better. Whether your child has been working with an occupational therapist for years or has just completed a sensory profile assessment, or if you are in the initial stages of researching SPD, this part of the book can help you better understand your child's behavioral difficulties. However, this book is not intended to replace a professional assessment. Your child should be assessed by an occupational therapist or pediatrician. The resources section on page 128 has a link to directories of competent and qualified occupational therapists.

Following the background information, the real fun begins. Part two walks you through sixty fun and engaging activities to help your child practice self-regulation and mindfulness. Each chapter includes twenty activities based on one of the three categories of arousal responses: sensory over-responsiveness, sensory under-responsiveness, and sensory seeking. The activities I share are ones I personally use to help children focus and be happy and calm. Where possible, I suggest ways to make toys and tools to facilitate sensory processing, but in several cases I recommend purchasing commercial items, like a Sit 'n' Spin or a trampoline. Several of the activities call for tools made from Lycra (an elastic fabric). Whatever the case may be, having a few of these sensory tools on hand can help you better help your child.

No matter what your experience with SPD, this book offers creative solutions to complex behaviors. I am thankful you are reading this book. Let me assure you that this is a great place to find ways to help promote self-regulation and mindfulness in your child.

Part
One

Sensory Processing Disorder & Self-Regulation

Ready, set, grow! Sensory processing and self-regulation impact everything we do, day and night. If I'm having an exciting time visiting with a friend, then I'm in a good place or "just right." If I'm nervous about an upcoming test or special project, then I'm "running high" in my self-regulation. If I've just eaten a huge and delicious lunch and I feel like taking a nap, then I'm running on "low." When I understand which arousal state I'm in, I can plan activities to help me stay at "just right" throughout the busy day. These terms—high, low, and just right—are used by the Alert Program, a curriculum that teaches self-regulation. They help us understand how sensory processing works in a concrete way to better help children with sensory processing disorder. These first three chapters explore sensory processing disorder, self-regulation, and mindfulness.

CHAPTER ONE

A Brief Introduction to SPD

Children with sensory processing disorder (SPD) are "out of sync," not only with their senses and their bodies, but also with their parents, teachers, and friends. In *The Out-of-Sync Child,* Carol Stock Kranowitz, MA, describes how children can become dysregulated as a result of how they interpret sensory input. Dysregulated children can have poor self-esteem, difficulties with coordination, and/or problems making friends. Helping children understand their bodies and how they learn makes life easier for them. Sensory-stimulating activities can help them better process incoming information and get back into sync with their environment, thereby restoring trust, discipline, and compliance. Helping your child understand and improve their sensory processing ability allows them to navigate their social world so that they can successfully embrace life.

What Is Sensory Processing Disorder?

According to the 1973 book *Sensory Integration and Learning Disorders* by A. Jean Ayres, sensory integration (SI) is "the involuntary process of the brain to assemble pictures of our environment at each moment in time using information from all of our senses. Through SI, the many parts of the nervous system work together so that a person can interact with their environment effectively and experience satisfaction." As science progressed, the term *sensory processing* replaced the term *sensory integration,* but they have the same meaning. Sensory processing disorder, therefore, is a condition in which the brain has difficulty receiving and responding to the information that comes through one or more senses.

The term *sensory processing disorder* is the diagnostic label for a problem with the way a person takes in, interprets, or responds to sensory stimuli. This is a very broad and descriptive diagnosis. Although occupational therapists and researchers continue to provide evidence for the validity of the diagnosis, the medical community has not yet officially recognized this diagnosis in the *Diagnostic and Statistical Manual of Mental Disorders* (DSM). The DSM is the manual medical providers use for coding diagnoses for insurance purposes. Currently, SPD is recognized in the *Diagnostic Classification of Mental Health and Developmental Disorders of Infancy and Early Childhood*. Most recently, the major self-regulation disorders, including attention-deficit/hyperactivity disorder, autism spectrum disorder, and obsessive-compulsive disorder, have been recognized by the medical community as having a sensory component.

To better understand sensory processing disorder, it's important to understand how humans learn about their environment through their senses. Let's take a quick look at the eight senses in basic terms to get an idea of the complex anatomy of these senses and how important they are to everyday functioning.

The Foreground Senses

There are five foreground senses: auditory (hearing), olfactory (smell), gustatory (taste), tactile (touch), and visual (sight). One is not more important than the other. Rather, what is important is that all of our senses work together in an integrated fashion. Let's take a look at each.

Auditory System (Hearing)

The structure of our ears provides us with the ability to hear sounds. Sound is then processed in the primary auditory cortex of the brain, which can detect sound frequency, amplitude, and other sound combinations. There are four basic reasons a person may experience difficulty hearing: a feeling of fullness in the ears, sudden hearing loss, fluctuating hearing loss accompanied by dizziness, and difficulty hearing people in a noisy environment (filtering). If you suspect your child has any of the first three symptoms, consult an audiologist for evaluation. However, if the problem is that your child can't focus in a noisy environment, you may be dealing with an auditory filtering issue, which can be a concern for people with SPD.

A Sensory Processing Analogy

Every human being uses sensory integration to function. This is how we take information from the world around us, process it through our brain, and tell our bodies to respond. A computer analogy can help simplify this complex neurological process: You receive input from the world through your eight senses, which act as your keyboard. The strokes on the keyboard send sensory information to the computer's central processing unit (CPU), your brain. The CPU takes this information, processes it into commands based on the needs of each system, and sends out commands to create the desired output, such as a printout or display (in this analogy, the printout or display is your behavior and movements). When you see the printout or display, you are provided with feedback on whether or not your input was effectively entered and processed. In real life, this creates a dynamic feedback loop, where the environment gives feedback to your brain on how the behavior or movement was received—if it was effective or ineffective, right or wrong.

Olfactory System (Smell)

How can we tell if something smells clean, dirty, rancid, or sweet? Scent processing is handled by the olfactory system, a highly sensitive sensory system. The sense of smell helps us filter out background smells and quickly identify and discriminate among different odors to keep us safe (fire, smoke, spoiled versus safe foods, etc). One's sense of smell highly impacts memory of traumatic events. In other words, people who have experienced trauma may recall the associated smell and relive the traumatic event. Children with SPD may have a hyperacute sense of smell. Their sensitivity to these background smells makes it hard for them to focus.

Gustatory System (Taste)

The gustatory system is responsible for how we perceive taste and flavor. The tongue has more than 10,000 taste buds, which detect sweet, sour, salty, and bitter flavors and send that information to the brain. Our sense of taste helps us discriminate between safe and harmful foods. The ability to detect sour tastes assists with survival in that it protects us from eating spoiled foods, rotten meats, and overripe fruit. Bitter tastes often are unpleasant and potentially dangerous. These could include nicotine, caffeine, and strychnine. Many medicines when chewed are bitter, and the body can interpret them as poisonous. Typically, children prefer salty and sweet foods to those that taste bitter or sour. This is because sugary foods release feel-good chemicals in the brain, and the crunch associated with salty foods brings a similar satisfaction. Children with SPD may have very strong food preferences, including specific cravings and foods that they avoid. This can often result in the child being referred to as a "picky eater," and makes eating a balanced diet difficult and stressful. In the chapters to come, "oral motor" activities will help children with SPD to further develop this sense.

Tactile System (Touch)

The sense of touch is called the tactile system. It processes touch information from the body, including pressure, temperature, and pain. Working with the tactile system is very important in the treatment of SPD. Tactile symptoms such as tactile over-responsiveness (defensiveness) or under-responsiveness are common in children with SPD. The tactile system is one of the three foundational systems used in sensory integration treatment (the other two are vestibular and proprioceptive senses, which I'll describe in the next section).

Visual System (Sight)

Our eyes detect light, which is necessary for vision. The sense of sight provides important information regarding safety, location, color, shape, and position/orientation, and if an object is static or in motion. Any distortion in the visual system results in a less-than-accurate interpretation of visual input to the brain. In addition to visual acuity, the visual system is also responsible for filtering (that is, helping the body understand brightness/glare). If you suspect your child has difficulty with vision, consult an optometrist. Other professionals such as ophthalmologists and behavioral optometrists are skilled at addressing visual difficulties.

One example of a visual perceptual disorder present with SPD is Irlen syndrome. This results in difficulty with the brain's ability to filter visual information. Symptoms of Irlen syndrome include headaches, migraines, light sensitivity, attention and concentration problems, difficulty with depth perception, and print distortions on a typed page. Irlen syndrome can make reading challenging and is treated with color transparency overlays or filtered lenses in glasses.

The Background Senses

There are three additional senses that help us understand and interact with the world. Because they work in the background, they are not as obvious as the foreground senses. We really don't know these senses are working unless we are having difficulty with them, as can be the case with SPD. The three background senses are proprioception, vestibular, and interoception. Even though these senses are hidden, they are extremely important to our well-being and ability to learn.

Proprioception

Proprioception is the sense of muscle and joints that tells you where your body is in space (body space awareness). It tells you the position, location, and orientation of the body and provides you with a sense of relative position within the body. The organs for this very important sense include the stretch receptors in your muscles and ligaments and the neurons in the inner ear. These neurons detect motion and orientation in space.

There are two basic types of body space awareness. The first is conscious proprioception; it involves any deliberate action resulting from your position in space. Conscious proprioception helps you walk up and down a hill, as your vision tells you where to place your foot and your proprioception sense tells you how to safely step as you walk. The second is unconscious proprioception, which tells you information about your body position without vision or other sensory input. Unconscious proprioception involves your reflexes and internal awareness without conscious effort. Unconscious proprioception is critical to the sensory aspect of improving sensory processing abilities.

Closely related to proprioception and tactile awareness is stereognosis, the ability to identify an object without using your eyes. It's important to be able to identify objects without looking. Imagine looking for a flashlight in your night table drawer during a power outage. How do you know if you have a flashlight versus a can of hairspray? The same skill is important when reaching into a purse to find your car keys. You'd generally stick your hand in to try to find them rather than open the purse wide to locate them visually.

In the chapters to come, you will see activities concentrating on "heavy work." Heavy work is any type of activity that pushes or pulls against the body. This helps children with SPD feel centered and grounded and engages proprioception.

Vestibular System

The vestibular system gives you a sense of where you are moving, whether you are balanced, and how you are oriented in space. It is important to know where you are moving for both safety and self-confidence. The planes of movement include forward and backward, from side to side, up and down, rotational/circular, and axial (rotating on an axis). These directions are measured by the position of the eustachian tubes in relation to the earth's gravity.

The eustachian tubes are the semicircular canal system in the inner ears that detects rotation. Otoliths detect linear acceleration and deceleration. When you move through space, the vestibular system sends a signal to the parts of the brain that control eye movements and keep you upright. There are three semicircular canals in the inner ear that lay at right angles to each other: the horizontal canal (detects rotation on a vertical axis), the anterior canal (detects movement in the forward/backward plane), and the posterior canal (detects movement in a frontal plane). Together the canals allow you to sense rotation in all directions.

The vestibular system is highly reliant on several parts of the brain. In general terms, this includes the cerebellum, which detects movements of the head, eyes, and posture; three cranial nerves that permit eyes to fix on a moving object while staying in focus; the reticular formation, which signals how to adjust circulation and breathing when the body moves; the spinal cord, which allows quick reflex reactions for balance; and the thalamus to control the head and body motor responses.

Interoception

Interoception is one of the newer senses to become popular in sensory processing theory. This sense has, of course, always been present in humans, but it is only now being discussed and better understood. Interoception includes any of the senses that detect conditions within the body, such as hunger, thirst, fatigue, and the need to use the bathroom. (You may come across a similar-sounding word, *enteroception*, in the dictionary, but this is a different process.) The sense of feeling hot or cold internally is also known through interoception. In addition, the sense of sexual arousal (both pleasurable and uncomfortable) arises here.

This sense may be less intense than other senses so it's easier to ignore. For example, a child may completely ignore the need to use the bathroom while they are playing a video game. They become so hyperfocused on the visual input that the internal need to go is lessened—until it becomes critical or they have an accident.

Neurologically, interoception is detected through nerve endings lining the respiratory and digestive mucous membranes. It works closely with the vestibular system and proprioceptive sense to inform a person about their body. This can include becoming sweaty, cramps/muscle spasms (pinching internally), and even pain. When all systems are functioning normally, a person can feel interoception, proprioception, and vestibular input accurately, which is important for interacting with the world.

What's Your Child's Sensory Profile?

A child with SPD must work a lot harder to interpret the many demands of their environment. Sensory processing is a normal mechanism we all experience, and we can all have good days and bad days. However, a child with SPD can have such intense sensitivities to sensory inputs that they interfere with normal life.

Children with SPD show a pattern of repeatedly struggling with the same issue (eating, dressing, playing, school, relationships, etc.) over a period to the degree that it affects their day-to-day functioning. For instance, a child with SPD may have difficulty filtering the sunshine on the playground, which may cause them to seek out movement; this urge to move could cause them to climb too high and become frightened by the height, resulting in a need for help to get down. They may not remember to tell you they went somewhere else on the playground because their impulse to move is so great that safety is forgotten. Socially, this child may crave movement so much that they can't wait to take a turn in a game or, academically, can't sit still to learn classroom lessons.

Like the child described, your child with SPD likely has behavioral patterns and characteristics that interfere with their daily activities. Many of these characteristics can be grouped into three categories of arousal responses to everyday sensory inputs:

- Sensory over-responsive

- Sensory under-responsive

- Sensory seeking

In a classroom, a child who is sensory over-responsive may be stressed out visually by the overhead fluorescent lighting. The lights trigger a stress response where they want to run, scream, or "misbehave." Children with sensory under-responsiveness may appear tired and disconnected, especially when they need to pay attention. This child may slouch in a chair. The teacher may interpret this poor posture as lazy, not paying attention, or slacking off. Instead, this child just needs more stimulation to benefit from the lesson. A child who is sensory seeking will fidget and may fall out of their chair at times. This child may wiggle, constantly move, and make funny sounds. All three students need something different from the teacher and the environment in order to be able to focus and learn.

If you haven't done so already, an occupational therapist can complete a comprehensive assessment of your child's sensory processing abilities. One result may be a sensory profile, which lists how your child processes sensory information. If your child does not have a sensory profile or similar report, see the resources on page 128 for a link to a directory of occupational therapists who are trained and experienced in SPD. The results of a sensory profile assessment can help you as well as your child's therapist choose specific activities that can help the most.

In the next chapter, we'll look at each of these profiles in more depth. It is possible for your child to display characteristics in all three categories. This is why it's so important to understand your child's unique sensory profile before implementing sensory activities at home.

CHAPTER TWO

Self-Regulation

At times, most children feel dysregulated and need help regaining their composure. They may become tired and cranky, have meltdowns, and cry in seemingly nonthreatening situations. Kids with SPD feel this way a lot of the time, which makes dealing with everyday life harder. Their self-regulation is off. Luckily, self-regulation can be taught. When a person achieves self-regulation, they feel grounded and experience homeostasis, a state of stability. Being self-regulated allows them to rise to the challenge of new tasks, take risks, and feel a sense of internal peace. That's a wonderful outcome for one very complex process! In this chapter, let's dive deeper into this concept of self-regulation and how activity and sensory input promote a sense of well-being and groundedness.

What Is Self-Regulation?

Self-regulation is the ability to manage emotions, thoughts, behavior, and body movement when faced with a situation that's tough to handle, enabling us to interact and participate in everyday activities. This complex process involves a coordinated effort between one's physical, emotional, neurological, and behavioral systems. The ability to self-regulate is generally learned from primary caregivers in the first few years of life. Self-regulation can also be taught through activities that involve vestibular and proprioceptive feedback, as well as auditory, visual, oral, and tactile input. These self-regulation activities can help your child with SPD feel better and more able to handle daily stresses.

Recall the three main categories of sensory processing disorders introduced in the previous chapter: sensory over-responsive, sensory under-responsive, and sensory seeking.

Children with sensory over-responsiveness are more sensitive to stimulation than most people. Their bodies feel sensation too easily or too intensely. A child with sensory over-responsiveness reacts by withdrawing from the activity as they try to self-regulate. For example, this child will disproportionately overreact when painting and getting messy. This child may refuse to put their hands in the paint. If they are coaxed to get messy, they immediately need to clean their hands. This child may wipe or rub the messy spot and even have a meltdown. Withdrawing, obsessive behavior, wiping and rubbing, and throwing a tantrum are ways the child attempts to self-regulate. Other characteristics may include picky eating, being fearful of certain sounds, and avoiding group activities. Even if it isn't a productive or desired response, the child will continue this behavior until something else happens (e.g., the sensory input from messy hands is reduced, understood, or a helpful adult intervenes). This child may overreact to everyday sensory input such as a touch or hug and pull away, which can affect relationships. One child I worked with would only hug sideways. However, after occupational therapy, the child began to tolerate full-body hugs.

Children who are sensory under-responsive are often quiet and passive, and disregard stimuli available in their environment. This child takes longer to register a sensory event. Their under-responsivity may lead to poor body awareness, clumsiness, or awkward movements. They may appear lethargic and slow to get going. For example, these children are accident-prone and fall when they aren't paying full attention to where they are walking. Parents can find it quite frustrating that their child is always falling; it may appear that the child is avoiding the situation by falling out of their chairs or laughing in stressful situations. They need more input to self-regulate. They need activities to be bigger, brighter, faster, and more interesting. This child may do better in a more spontaneous and chaotic environment. They may benefit from sitting near extremely social children and other sources of sound.

A child who is sensory seeking actively seeks stimulation and may have an insatiable desire for sensory input. These children excessively seek out stimulation, always crashing, bumping, chewing, pushing, wiggling, and jiggling. For example, a child who is "always on the go" will move, climb, and wiggle a lot, perhaps compromising their safety. Parents may become frustrated that their child seems to never get tired, no matter how long they stay at the park. This child will benefit from fidget toys and tactilely diverse material. At times, this child should sit on a therapy ball, complete isometric activities, and do "chair sit-ups" that provide proprioception (a sense of movement and body position) and heavy work without being distracting.

Please remember, it is not the intention to label or box your child into a specific sensory category. It is possible for your child to display characteristics in all three categories. Many children do. This is why it's so important to understand your child's unique sensory profile before implementing sensory activities at home.

Will Medication Help?

Medicating a child is a very personal decision that many parents struggle with. If your child's pediatrician recommends medication, investigate behavioral and/or sensory processing interventions before making your decision. In general, children with SPD should be treated by an occupational therapist. Medication typically treats a specific area of the nervous system, not always the whole child. With that said, the decision on whether or not to medicate your child needs to be thoughtfully and individually made in conjunction with your child's doctor. When a parent does not want to put their child on medication or is unsure, I recommend working with an occupational therapist for six months to "clear up" sensitivities and then determine what other support the child may need.

How Are Self-Regulation Skills Taught?

Controlling their level of attention and behavior can be challenging for many children, but it can be learned with practice and repetition. Fun and motivating activities can be effective in promoting self-regulation, especially for children struggling with sensory issues. That's what this book is all about!

One of the ways I teach self-regulation is by using an analogy from the Alert Program to explain to children how to reach a "just right" state. You can explain it this way to your child, too: When your engine is running "just right," you have enough energy and focus to arrive at your destination (or accomplish your goals). If your car engine is running high, it's revving out of control or going too fast and you might get into an accident. If the car engine is running too slow, the car might run out of gas and not get you where you need to go. If you're running too high or too low, that's when you need to figure out what your car needs. With this analogy, your child can get an idea of how to recognize their "engine speed," and then you can offer strategies to help them change and maintain that speed to "just right."

In my clinic, I use a two-pronged approach to teaching self-regulation: I work from the inside out and the outside in. The inside-out approach involves trying to make permanent neurological changes to the child's nervous system. I do this with a series of very intensive sensory integration therapies, involving lots of vestibular, proprioception, and tactile input. I also use a variety of cognitive-behavioral approaches that integrate sensory techniques. In my clinic, a child plays games on swings or a jungle gym and engages in a variety of auditory, visual, and tactile activities. Sessions typically run fifty to sixty minutes once or twice a week. (The resources section on page 128 includes information on therapist-directed interventions so that you can become familiar with what's available.)

The outside-in approach involves engaging the child in the fun activities provided in this book. After a comprehensive evaluation, I prescribe a home program of safe and fun activities for the guardians, siblings, teachers, and/or other adults to implement. I firmly believe that guardians are integral to the success of teaching a child to self-regulate. The parent and caregivers need to implement the home program regularly throughout the week. My favorite activities integrate as many of the senses as possible. I also like activities that include other children. I especially want the child to try games that are challenging to their sensory sensitivities. In other words, if the child finds it easy to do something, the idea is to make it harder. In my clinic, I want the child to trust me enough to try the games that challenge the areas that are overwhelming, tough, and even scary. As you work with your child on self-regulating activities in a fun and engaging way, you'll find that your child's trust in you and the process grows.

The therapeutic games in part two of this book promote planning and problem-solving. These activities will help your child develop attention, sequencing, and motor planning skills. Calming techniques, self-awareness exercises, and mindfulness activities also support the development of self-regulation. Providing your child with activities that are the "just right" level of challenge can motivate them to try novel or hard tasks. This is why it's important to use fun activities rather than rote exercises.

What Is a Sensory Diet?

A sensory diet is a schedule of activities intentionally placed in a child's day that assists with arousal, attention, and their ability to function. The sensory diet is important to help a child with SPD feel organized and calm, so they can obtain an optimal state for learning, paying attention, and self-control. A sensory diet is similar to a diet focused on healthy eating in that it consists of activities aimed at helping your child feel more energetic, more grounded, and ready for whatever happens in their day.

Sensory diets consist of activities that are personalized to each child and include physical exercises that aid in self-regulation. Typically, an occupational therapist develops this plan based on their comprehensive assessment, and parents and teachers implement the diet. In my work in school-based occupational therapy, I set up regularly scheduled sensory diets for my students. Initially, I ask their teacher to allow rests from learning every thirty minutes and provide the child with a way to "let their wiggles out." This might include eating crunchy foods for snack, jumping on a trampoline, swinging, using a weighted blanket, or spending time in a sensory safe corner. In addition, I often prepare a waist pack containing smaller sensory tools for the child to carry around. This might include mouth toys, gum, and quiet hand fidgets.

CHAPTER THREE

Mindfulness

Mindfulness practice is an effective tool to help kids thrive in stressful situations and primes their brains and bodies to self-regulate. This can be true for any child, but for a child with SPD, it is especially important to develop this skill. In this chapter, I'll discuss what mindfulness is and how it affects the brain. I'll also discuss how learning to breathe and remain grounded helps children with SPD cope with their big emotions. When your child is feeling more grounded and focused on the here and now, they will feel more capable of addressing the challenges of day-to-day life.

What Is Mindfulness?

Mindfulness is a state of growing calm and grounded by focusing our awareness on the present moment. It involves noticing what our senses are picking up while engaging in any activity. It is a sense of relaxation while calmly acknowledging and accepting our feelings, thoughts, and body sensations. Yoga is one tool frequently used to practice mindfulness. In yoga, the term *monkey mind* is often used to describe an inner voice that distracts us throughout the day, giving us a running commentary about things to do, feelings, and "should-haves" and "could-haves." Monkey mind is also referred to as "the inner critic," or the unsettled, confused, and restless thoughts that sometimes occur when people get stressed out. While practicing mindfulness, distracting thoughts and feelings are not ignored but greeted and watched without judgment.

There are many benefits to practicing mindfulness with your child, including:

- Increased feelings of tranquility and being grounded

- An ability to deal more effectively with stress and anxiety

- Better focus and concentration

- An easier time handling big and difficult emotions

- Increased imagination and creativity

- An easier time falling asleep at night due to peaceful feelings

Mindfulness is much more than sitting still and meditating. Children need an active approach to the mindful meditation process. Often when I'm working with children with SPD, I notice they are in a stress state of fight, flight, or freeze. I help these children feel grounded by adding structure and safety to the process. I try to find activities that are engaging and meaningful. Initially, I guide children through a warm-up story or activity, then the actual mindfulness meditation, followed by discussion questions and a creative project. This helps children understand that mindfulness is a process.

How Does Mindfulness Affect the Brain?

There's a diverse body of research that connects mindfulness with positive changes in behavior, function, and structures in the brain. For example, in 2005, 225 children with a high level of anxiety, ages five to eight, were enrolled in an "Attention Academy Program" and trained in mindfulness techniques by researchers. The children attended twelve sessions for forty-five minutes each. At the end of the program, the children demonstrated a significant decrease in test anxiety and an increase in attention span. In 2010, other researchers examined children ages ten to thirteen with behavioral problems and depression before and after the children had engaged in mindfulness lessons three times a day. The results showed a significant reduction in behavioral problems and depression.

The results of these two studies are impressive, and the research on the benefits of mindfulness is constantly building. In fact, a team of researchers conducted a highly complex analysis of existing research studies on how mindfulness impacts the brain and published their findings in 2014. They examined brain-imaging studies and localized specific emotions to parts of the brain. Their analysis concluded that people who meditate often have less activity in the part of the brain where sensation and emotion are processed. Therefore, people who practiced mindfulness are less impacted by emotions, stress, and fear.

Mindfulness induces a relaxation response by engaging the parasympathetic nervous system (the "rest and repair" part of the autonomic nervous system) and helps restore the body after a stressful experience. Heart rate, respiratory rate, blood pressure, and muscle tension decrease, as does the production of cortisol and other stress hormones; this minimizes the physical symptoms of stress and decreases the risk of high blood pressure, heart problems, insomnia, and persistent fatigue.

How Can Mindfulness Help a Child with SPD?

Children with SPD often have huge reactions to everyday occurrences and can make too much out of a minor issue. It is hard for these children to deal with intense emotions because their sensory processing issues, whatever they may be, can interfere with the development of healthy coping strategies. That's why being mindful is an especially powerful self-regulation tool for kids with SPD. There are many ways to attain a mindful presence throughout the day. Here are a few examples:

- Be silent to hear and be aware of your surroundings
- Breathe consciously by inhaling and exhaling deeply
- Listen to the notes of slow, quiet music
- Make gentle movements to calm and settle jitters
- Walk in nature
- Work in a garden
- Practice yoga

Mindfulness practices that you can teach to your child include meditation, yoga, and deep-breathing techniques. Don't worry if you don't know how to do these things yet. I'll provide you with instructions in part two.

One neat aspect of mindfulness is that it can be practiced anywhere at any time. Aside from yoga, where comfortable, stretchy clothing is best, there are no specific requirements for environment, clothing, or body position. Yes, it is easier to relax in a quiet and calm environment, but anyone can practice breathing consciously no matter where they are. It's also possible to do simple yoga stretches and meditate in a busy room, a noisy classroom, or even on the playground. All that's required is the ability to calm and center oneself to the point of relaxation. It becomes easier with consistent practice.

Many of the children I work with are anxious, stressed, or sad. Mindfulness is a powerful tool to help children who feel this way. That's why I integrate it into my practice. For example, Charlie, an eight-year-old boy, was looking at a test he had failed. He began to laugh and fell on the floor. This response did not make sense. Charlie wasn't happy about failing. He just didn't know how to process the big emotions of confusion, embarrassment, and fear. I taught him basic yoga moves and deep-breathing exercises, which helped him get less upset and gave him a way to respond when his engine was running too high. He enjoyed the stronger standing and balance poses because they helped him clear his mind and focus.

In another case, Emma was sent home from school because she was biting other children. When her classmates teased her, she would often bite them. In occupational therapy, she learned how to relax with alternate-nostril breathing (see Calm Breathing on page 110) and created a social story using guided visual imagery. Now when Emma gets upset, she pulls out her story, reads it, and walks away from the children who are upsetting her. She worked with her teachers, who taught her how to assertively address her classmates; the teachers also spoke with the other children to stop the bullying. With these tools, her feelings no longer escalated to the point where she wanted to bite.

Mindfulness is a powerful tool that results in lower stress and greater compassion, improved ability to focus, and an easier time connecting with others. In chapters four, five, and six, you'll find easy-to-learn techniques that you can use with your child. Learning these techniques takes only a short time, and putting in some practice each day can have lasting effects.

Part
Two

Self-Regulation Activities

Targeted activities give children with SPD the opportunity to explore their world and improve their sensory processing abilities. There are times when rote exercise is used to strengthen core muscles and practice specific movements, but for the most part, these activities provide the richness and fun aspect of learning a new skill.

Even the most engaging activities will sometimes be met with resistance. Should you force your child to play? My answer is a qualified no. Forcing a child with SPD to do something they are avoiding does no good. However, look closer at the activity and figure out why your child is refusing. Is it too hard? Is a stressful reaction happening because the activity is threatening or overwhelming? On the other hand, is this simply a way for your child to avoid doing something hard? Whatever the answer, use your knowledge of your child to reengage them by making the same activity easier or less threatening, or offering an activity with similar benefits.

Most activities involving sensory input can be adapted to fit the individual sensory needs of your child. For example, if your child is sensory under-responsive, they will benefit from activities in which they spin quickly and in circular patterns on a swing that rotates in all directions. However, if your child is sensory over-responsive, they will benefit more from gentle back-and-forth swinging. If your child is sensory seeking, they will like swinging in all planes, quickly, and in unpredictable patterns. All three types of SPD may benefit from the same type of activity but with different approaches. You'll find safe and engaging activities for children who are sensory over-responsive in chapter four, for children who are sensory under-responsive in chapter five, and for children who are sensory seeking in chapter six.

Remember, these activities are not a substitute for occupational therapy. Instead, take these ideas as simple ways to meet your child's sensory needs at home or, if you are a teacher, in a school setting. If your child is attending structured therapy with a licensed practitioner, be sure to follow their instructions. These activities should be fun and engaging, and within your child's ability level, but they should also slightly challenge them to grow.

CHAPTER FOUR

Activities for Sensory Over-Responsiveness

Children with sensory over-responsiveness are more sensitive to stimulation than most people. Their bodies feel sensation too easily or too intensely. The child reacts by withdrawing, engaging in obsessive behavior such as wiping and rubbing or throwing tantrums as they try to self-regulate. The child will continue this behavior until something else happens (for example, the sensory input is reduced, understood, or a helpful adult intervenes).

The key to helping your over-responsive child is twofold: change the nervous system or change the environment. Changing the child's nervous system is a hard task, especially as the child gets older; it involves rewiring the child's nervous system over time, calming them down so that activities and environments no longer cause an extreme response to the sensory input. With this change, a child with tactile defensiveness would finally be able to tolerate wearing new clothes or having their hair washed. On the other hand, changing the environment means decreasing or increasing the sensory stimuli so that the child can better function. For example, turning down overhead lights may help a child tolerate visual input. Often, environmental changes are simple to make and decrease stress.

The sooner your sensory over-responsive child starts intervention, the better the results. If your child's behavior and functioning cause undue stress and they are showing signs of poor self-esteem, it's time to ask a professional for assistance if you haven't already done so. With that said, these activities are fun to do at home, and most can be done with minimal equipment.

Eat It or Wear It Challenge

This game is a fun challenge for picky eaters. The child gets to choose whether to try a food or put it somewhere on their body. For example, if the child reaches into a bag and pulls out a green bean, they can choose to either eat the green bean or place it over their ear. This is especially fun with two or more players. Be prepared to get messy!

ACTIVITY TYPE: Gustatory, Messy play, Oral motor, Tactile

What You'll Need:

- Two or more food items (preferred and not preferred) for each participant
- Paper bags (at least 2 per participant)
- Index cards (at least 2 per participant)

Directions:

1. Before beginning, place each food item in a separate paper bag. Number the bags and the index cards sequentially so that each bag has a matching index card. Place the index cards facedown.

2. The child draws a numbered index card, reaches into the corresponding bag, and pulls out the food item.

3. The child decides whether they will eat or wear the food.

4. Participants continue to take turns until all the bags have been opened and the food has either been eaten or worn.

David: Picky Eating Habits

David is a fun-loving, generally happy six-year-old boy. He does well in first grade, except when it comes to eating. Initially, he ate anything offered, but around eighteen months old, he started to develop picky eating habits. He currently does not like his food to touch other foods and needs a plate with dividers. While he does not exhibit signs of tactile defensiveness, he needs a lot of touching and cuddling for reassurance. He has major meltdowns if he's forced to eat vegetables, and he will only eat one type of chicken nugget.

His parents have tried everything, and they are upset that he won't eat normally. They have him assessed by an occupational therapist and find out he's orally defensive and tactile seeking (sensory over-responsive to oral input and sensory under-responsive to tactile input). The home program includes an invitation to the "Eat It or Wear It Challenge." The week before the event, David's parents help him practice. They let him choose his favorite foods to either eat or put on part of his body. He also practices with green vegetables. He typically enjoys this game.

During the actual event, he sits with three other children at the table, and each one takes a turn choosing a bag. The kids pick a bag, open it up, and decide whether they want to eat it or wear it. When it is David's turn, he chooses to eat one item and wear the other. Overall, this silly game makes him happy and he enjoys watching his friends eat or wear the food as well. He's willing to play again with different foods.

Human Sling

Children enjoy being swung by trusted adults in this makeshift swing. This activity is calming and helps the over-responsive child focus.

ACTIVITY TYPE: Core strength, Heavy work, Proprioception, Vestibular

SAFETY TIP: The weight of the child should be within the range that two strong adults can comfortably lift in the sheet.

What You'll Need:

- Crash pad or pillows (for safety)
- An old, clean sheet
- Two strong adults

Directions:

1. Place the crash pad or pillows on the floor, and spread out the sheet.

2. Ask the child to pick a command to stop the game if they don't want to continue once you get started, and then invite the child to lie down in the middle of the sheet.

3. Each adult picks up the 2 corners of the sheet on their side, creating a sling, and lifts the sheet and child off the floor. The adults swing the child back and forth.

4. If the child says to stop the activity (or when the game naturally concludes), gently place the sling down and allow the child to climb out.

VARIATIONS: Give a child with sensory under-responsiveness more sensory input by pulling the child along the floor in the sheet. Also, one child can pull another child along the floor in the sheet, as this provides lots of heavy work.

Cocoon

This game allows the child to experience gentle circular swinging while being enclosed in a teardrop-shaped swing, as if in a cocoon. Circular swinging may be threatening to an over-responsive child, so the enclosed nature of this type of swing provides them with a feeling of safety and comfort. The cushion is typically soft and gives extra input for vestibular sense and balance. I also use this activity for kids who are gravitationally insecure. These children don't like their feet to leave the ground, but they feel safe when surrounded by the soft cloth walls.

ACTIVITY TYPE: Proprioception, Vestibular, Visual tracking

SAFETY TIPS: Child should be under 75 pounds. Only use this swing with the child sitting inside with legs crisscrossed.

What You'll Need:

- A commercially available indoor teardrop-shaped swing (Lycra is best) or other net swing of similar shape that allows movement forward and backward, from side to side, circular (spins on axis), and rotational (spins to carve out a circle)

Directions:

1. Invite the child to climb into the swing and sit crisscross on the swing seat. (No standing up.)

2. Place a heavy blanket or heavy toy on the child's lap. This provides gentle pressure on the child, which may be calming.

3. If the child wants to be fully cocooned, put the blanket over the child's head so they are covered but can still peek out.

4. Start with very gentle side-to-side swinging. Gradually change the movement to forward and backward.

5. Gently move the swing in circular motion, round and round. Make it fun and relaxing by singing a song or counting the number of times they rotate.

TIP: I highly recommend having a Lycra teardrop-shaped swing in your home for your child with SPD. This type of swing can be installed with relative ease following the manufacturer's instructions and shouldn't take up a lot of room.

Swing Safety

Suspended toys that are safe, sturdy, and soundly built provide fun, directly activate both the vestibular and proprioceptive systems, and improve core strength. When hanging a swing at home, be sure to purchase a sturdy swing swivel (a rotational device) that can be firmly anchored. A swing swivel allows the swing to move forward and backward, from side to side, and in rotation. This type of movement promotes vestibular sense, proprioception, and visual tracking. It is especially good for over-responsive children, as the swinging motion can be kept gentle. Under-responsive children often like that the swing swivel can make the swing go faster.

Movement in all planes is important for the development of vestibular sense. How you determine the direction of movement is relative to the position of your child's eustachian tubes. For example, if your child is sitting upright, the motion is measured from a vertical position. If your child is lying down, the motion is measured from a horizontal position.

Here are a few safety precautions when using swings:

- Use the swing as it's intended. If it's a sitting swing, only sit on the seat.

- Be sure the swing is stopped completely before getting off. Slide off feet first.

- Only one child at a time on the swing; make sure one child is off before another child gets on.

- Watch out for tripping hazards near the swing (other toys, back-packs, etc.).

CONTINUED

- Be careful that other children do not run in front of a moving swing.

- Swings should be regularly inspected for safety, construction, fit, and wear and tear.

- Stay off wet swings, which can be slippery.

- Outdoor metal swings may be hot in the summer.

- Watch your child for signs of overstimulation. Look for skin color, sweating, and overall mood to make sure the child is not too dizzy and is still having fun. If the child is not having fun, stop and reintroduce it later. Respect the "no." If they've had enough swinging, stop the swing.

  When it comes to swings, what matters most is the child's ability to use them safely and the adult's ability to safely supervise. For example, I generally keep children off swings if they weigh more than 95 pounds because I can't safely spot them. Heavier children are harder to catch and keep safe. Younger children who are not yet walking are also harder to support. A younger child might enjoy a swing with more support (for example, a teardrop-shaped Lycra swing or net swing). A toddler could get on a horizontal platform swing, as long as they are safe to sit or lie down.

Tunnel Through

Pop-up play tunnels are a fun way for children to crawl, scoot, and explore. This game is ideal for children who want less sensory input. However, children who are under-responsive or sensory seeking also enjoy this game.

ACTIVITY TYPE: Heavy work, Total body strength, Vestibular

What You'll Need:

- Commercially available pop-up play tunnel
- Ball (optional)
- Beanbag (optional)

Directions:

1. Open the tunnel on a clear surface (gym floor, outdoor playground, gym mat, or carpeted floor).
2. Invite the child to crawl through the tunnel, first forward and then backward.
3. For more input, have the child push a ball (playground ball or heavier weighted ball) through with their head.
4. Provide a challenge by having the child balance a bean bag on their back while crawling through.

TIP: Tunnels with a hard side give more vestibular input (through the rocking). A hard-sided tunnel with wire structure will compact for easy storage. Easy pop-up tunnels are fun and portable. In its compact position, this toy is a flat, round object easily stored on the floor or in the back of a closet. Tunnels are relatively inexpensive, but they can also be made by hand (see page 72).

Two-Legged Fun

This imaginative activity allows the child to pretend to be an animal. These particular animal walks require the upper body and lower body to make different movements. Of course, a favorite part of this activity is to imitate the animal noise, so don't forget to add the sounds that animal makes.

ACTIVITY TYPE: Cardiovascular workout, Heavy work, Proprioception, Total body strength

What You'll Need:

- Gym mats (optional)
- Comfortable, loose clothing that can get dirty
- Gloves (optional)

Directions:

1. Do the horse gallop. Have the child stand upright and gallop forward like a horse. This requires stepping forward with the right leg and then hopping the left leg forward to meet the right, and continuing this way across the room. Encourage the child to neigh.

2. Do the bunny hop. Have the child stand upright with both feet together and bend their elbows so that their hands come up to their shoulders. Keeping both feet together, the child will hop forward. Their hands will naturally flop up and down. After hopping in a straight line, suggest the child hop from side to side, then quickly, slowly, and in a crisscross pattern. Encourage the child to make the sound of a bunny nibbling on a carrot.

3. Do the frog jump. Have the child crouch on all fours. Next, have them hop forward by extending their lower body, and then returning to the initial crouching position to complete the hop. Encourage the child to ribbit while hopping.

4. Do the duck waddle. Have the child squat down so that their feet are on the floor but their body is upright. The child first steps forward with their right foot and then their left foot while still squatting. They shouldn't let their hands touch the ground but can adjust their feet to remain upright as they waddle forward. Encourage the child to quack.

Slither and Slide

Kids really enjoy crawling and slithering on the floor. This activity allows the child to slink around on the ground by using their arms and legs to propel forward. This game is made more challenging by placing a weighted blanket over the child. Moving while under a weighted blanket can be calming. The weight makes the child work hard to pull their body along the floor.

ACTIVITY TYPE: Cardiovascular workout, Deep pressure, Heavy work, Total body strength

What You'll Need:

- Painter's tape

- Mats or carpeted floor

- A weighted blanket that comfortably covers the child (at least 4 by 5 feet) and weighs at least 10 percent of the child's body weight. If you plan to use it on a bed, be sure it fits the size of the bed. If you are going to use the blanket for lying on the floor or couch, be sure it's 1 to 2 feet longer than the child is high and at least 1 to 2 feet wider.

Directions:

1. Using painter's tape, create a course with curves and corners about 20 to 30 feet long for the child to follow.

2. Invite the child to lie on the floor on their tummy and instruct them to slither forward like a snake, using their hands and feet to propel forward. Encourage the child to keep their body as flat as possible, while raising their bottom or trunk off the floor.

3. Stand about 10 to 15 feet into the course and have the child slither forward to reach you. When they do, cover the child's body with a weighted blanket. Have the child continue along the course while keeping the blanket on top of them.

4. You can add a competitive element by timing how long it takes the child to slither along the whole course.

TIP: Two children can have a "slithering" race to the end of the course.

Where's Your Body?

Over-responsive children need help regulating strong emotions and behaviors. They are often wiggly and won't sit still. They may be overly sensitive to touch and need deep pressure input to settle down. This poor sense of body awareness may make it hard for them to recognize where their body is in space, making them clumsy and accident-prone. This game gives a child extra proprioceptive input from the weighted blanket, which promotes calming and focus. It also gives them a fun way to identify where their body is in space without using their eyes.

ACTIVITY TYPE: Deep pressure, Mindfulness, Proprioception

What You'll Need:

- A quiet room free of distractions (no TV or distracting noises in the background)

- A weighted blanket that comfortably covers the child (at least 4 by 5 feet) and weighs at least 10 percent of the child's body weight. If you plan to use it on a bed, be sure it fits the size of the bed. If you are going to use the blanket for lying on the floor or couch, be sure it's 1 to 2 feet longer than the child is high and at least 1 to 2 feet wider.

Directions:

1. Invite the child to lie on their back on a comfortable surface. This can be their bed, a mat on the floor, or on the couch. Cover them with the blanket, leaving their head uncovered.

2. Lead the child through focused breathing (see Calm Breathing on page 110 or Rectangle Breathing on page 47).

3. Touch the child's limbs through the blanket in different places. For example, put deep pressure on their ankle and hold it for 5 to 10 seconds. Ask the child to name where they felt the pressure.

4. Touch a hand, elbow, shoulder, ear, toe, ankle, or knee. Do not press down on the trunk area of the body. Alternate between right and left sides of the body so the child has to think about both sides. (If the child is ticklish, press with firmer pressure.)

5. Have the child roll over onto their tummy and continue the game.

Red Light/Green Light in Your Seat

Children who are sensory over-responsive need to be in continuous motion, so sitting still in a chair can be extremely hard for them. This game involves a sit disc, which can give the child's nervous system what it needs while still providing structure to help the child sit still.

ACTIVITY TYPE: Proprioception, Vestibular

What You'll Need:

- A sit disc (commercially available in a variety of colors and textures)
- A well-fitting chair for the child
- A desk
- A stack of tokens (or keep track of points on paper)

Directions:

1. Place the sit disc on the chair. Invite the child to sit on it, making sure they can place their feet flat on the floor and support themselves with the desk if needed.

2. Explain the game. When you say, "Green light," they can move, wiggle, bounce, and laugh, etc., as long as they remain seated. When you say, "Red light," they need to freeze and stop wiggling. Like the classic game, you will turn your back during green light and turn around during red light.

3. If the child remains still for at least 30 seconds after red light, they get a token. If the child moves during red light, they must give back a token. (It helps to start them out with a few tokens to begin). When your child earns 10 tokens, they win the game.

TIP: Be sure the child can sit in the chair safely and correctly. A well-fitting chair will allow the child to rest their feet on the floor, with their ankles, knees, and hips at 90 degrees. The desk should meet the child at mid-chest level, so their arms can rest on the desk with elbows bent at 90 degrees.

The Infinity Walk

The Infinity Walk helps a child progressively develop coordination. This walk allows the child to use their whole body and practice visual tracking. Children with SPD often have a poor ability to visually track objects, especially while moving. This activity has the child practice bilateral coordination. The brain is involved in coordination of both the upper and lower body doing different tasks, while focusing on visual stimuli. The motor, sensory, perceptual, cognitive, emotional, and relational habits of the child improve and are easy to monitor using this walking pattern.

ACTIVITY TYPE: Proprioception, Vestibular, Visual tracking

What You'll Need:

- A clear, open space for walking, free of obstacles (indoors or outdoors)

- Painter's tape

- Six toy traffic cones

Directions:

1. Affix painter's tape to the ground to create an infinity sign that is at least 10 by 6 feet. Place cones at the numbered sections (see diagram).

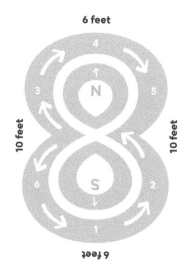

6 feet

10 feet

10 feet

6 feet

2. Have the child start at 1 and walk around the cones sequentially—1 through 6. This first round they should walk normally around the numbers for familiarization at least 3 times.

3. Now stand to the right of the intersecting lines about 4 feet away. This point should be visible from all parts of the Infinity Walk.

4. As the child walks around the cones, instruct them to maintain eye contact with you at all times. This requires their feet to walk on the line and their eyes to remain focused on you. You can talk with the child, walking them through the steps to encourage them to maintain eye contact. Have them do this 3 times.

TIP: Three times around the course should be sufficient each time a new task is added. You want the child to be familiar enough with the task to be able to master the route, but not stay on task for so long that it gets boring.

Crawling Obstacle Course

Kids love to be part of an obstacle course. The idea is to create simple steps that require children to move through obstacles in fun and challenging ways, have them memorize the steps in order, and then go through them in a timed manner. Obstacle courses are fun inside or outside. This course involves crawling over, under, and through objects.

ACTIVITY TYPE: Heavy work, Proprioception, Vestibular

What You'll Need:
- Clutter-free, non-distracting space (indoors or outdoors)
- Mats or blankets
- Two sturdy chairs
- Play tunnel
- Crash pad or cushions

Directions:
1. Create the obstacle course in a square with 1 task per corner. Put the resting spot at corner 1. This can be a mat or blanket to sit on. In corner 2, place two chairs side by side so that the child can crawl between the chairs or through the legs if the chairs have the space. In corner 3, place a play tunnel for crawling through or a blanket they need to crawl under from one side to the other. In corner 4, place the crash pad or cushions for the child to crawl over.

2. Initially, have the child practice each obstacle separately so they understand the instructions. The child should only be crawling to gain strength and endurance.

3. Next instruct them to crawl from corner 1 to corners 2, 3, and 4.

4. When this becomes easy, give the child verbal instructions on the order to complete the course. For example, have them go from corner 4 to corners 3, 2, and 1. Watch how the child's memory is used to navigate the course.

TIP: To make this more challenging, have the child crawl backward or sideways, or add additional steps to the course.

Chew Hard, Chew Soft

The mouth provides endless possibilities for calming. Many people put things in their mouth to calm down. This activity helps your child choose appropriate items that will help with calming. This activity includes food, but it is not meant to substitute for a meal, as these aren't a great source of calories. The point of this game is for the child to use their mouth to change their level of self-regulation. The child explores items that require a lot of chewing or a little bit of chewing. This helps them describe and understand how items in their mouth feel.

ACTIVITY TYPE: Gustatory, Oral motor, Proprioception

What You'll Need:

- Foods that are crunchy and hard to chew, such as gum (I prefer old Bazooka bubble gum because it's tough to chew), granola, nuts, popcorn, beef jerky, carrots, celery, cucumbers, licorice, Red Hots, etc. (See Tip on page 44.)

- Nonfood chewing items such as mouth toys, Chewy Tubes, chewy necklace, and pacifier

- Paper bag

- Napkins

- Trash bag

Directions:

1. Place all the food and nonfood items in a paper bag without showing them to the child. Have your child wash and dry their hands.

2. Model the steps of this game. Put your hand in the paper bag and choose one item from the bag. Name the item. Describe the characteristics of the item, including color, smell, sound (if any), and texture. Is it bendable, hard, soft, or squishy? Then take a bite if it's food or chew on the mouth toy. Use big, loud, chomping motions with your mouth open. Be sure to exaggerate the mouth chewing. (This isn't a game where manners count!) Now decide whether you had to chew hard or soft. Say whether or not you enjoyed the experience.

CONTINUED

3. Have the child pick out an item from the bag. Have them examine it and describe the color, smell, sound, and texture. Ask the child to lick it and describe the taste. Is it salty, sweet, sour, tart, or spicy? If it's a mouth toy, does it taste like plastic?

4. Ask the child to chew away. Let them know it's okay to chew loudly with their mouth open. Encourage them to *chomp, chomp, chomp!* (If it's a food they don't like, they can spit it out into the trash bag rather than swallow it.)

5. Have the child describe whether or not they enjoyed the food or chewing on the mouth toy. Did they need to chew hard or soft?

6. Alternate between taking a turn and having the child take a turn until the paper bag is empty.

TIP: It's okay to use a few sugar-based items for this game, but make sure you aren't mainly offering candy. The idea here is to stimulate chewing and crunching on various food items.

Swinging Alphabet

This is a variation of the Cocoon activity (page 32) and combines gentle swinging with learning. The child should be able to identify the letters of the alphabet or at least be able to sing the alphabet song. The swing allows the child to feel movement forward and backward, from side to side, circular (spins on axis), and rotational (spins to carve out a circle) while identifying the letters on the flash cards.

ACTIVITY TYPE: Proprioception, Vestibular, Visual tracking

SAFETY TIPS: Child should be under 75 pounds. Only use this swing with the child sitting inside with legs crisscrossed.

What You'll Need:

- A commercially available indoor teardrop-shaped swing or other net swing of similar shape that allows movement forward and backward, from side to side, circular, and rotational (spins to carve out a circle) (or see Alternative Equipment below)

- Twenty-six flash cards (one for each letter of the alphabet)

Directions:

1. Invite the child to sit inside the swing, safely, with legs crisscrossed. (No standing up.)

2. Swing the child in circles, holding up a flash card for each rotation. As the child sees the letter on the flash card, they call it out and you switch to the next letter for the next rotation.

3. At first, the child may not be able to tolerate all the rotations, so go slow. Be sure to keep the rhythm slow enough for the child to identify the letter, but keep the game gently competitive. Eventually, the child will be able to tolerate all 26 rotations in the game.

ALTERNATIVE EQUIPMENT: If you don't have a swing, this activity can be done using a Sit 'n' Spin, a computer chair, or another toy that rotates. The downside is that there are no soft walls for the added sense of security.

Gayle: Gravitational Insecurity

Six-year-old Gayle just began kindergarten. She's very smart and knows all her letters and numbers. However, she is afraid to play on the playground equipment. She stays away from games involving climbing on the jungle gym and monkey bars. When Gayle plays on them, she gets scared, cries, and runs away.

Gayle's parents took her to an occupational therapist, who tested her vestibular system. The results revealed that Gayle has gravitational insecurity. Her vestibular system is over-responsive, and she gets panicky when her feet leave the ground. Gayle now attends weekly therapy at a private practice OT clinic where her therapist uses a variety of swinging activities, including Swinging Alphabet. Her therapist also recommended her parents give her as much vestibular input as possible in a fun and natural way.

Gayle's parents purchased a three-foot trampoline. Gayle's dog, Sadie, immediately jumped on the trampoline, which made Gayle laugh. When Sadie hopped off, Gayle climbed on and started jumping, feeling safe because she could jump while still being close to the ground.

Gayle also lives in a neighborhood with a community park that has a jungle gym with a swing set. Gayle was hesitant to get on the swing, so her dad got on first and Gayle helped push him. Then she took a turn. They took frequent visits to the park. Then, for her birthday, Gayle and her friends had a picnic at the park near the jungle gym area. She and her friends all had fun on the jungle gym, and Gayle's parents were delighted.

Rectangle Breathing

Breathing is important for overall calmness. This is especially important for the child on the go. Breathing helps calm nervousness, center the body, and slow down the child. Often sensory over-responsive children need assistance settling down. One neat aspect of this activity is that you can do it anywhere. It's easier to relax in a quiet space with dim lighting; however, it's possible to practice breathing while sitting in a chair right before meals, before exercising, or during a family outing.

ACTIVITY TYPE: Mindfulness

What You'll Need:

- A quiet room with dim lights free of distractions (no TV or distracting noises in the background)

- A 7-by-10-inch rectangle (with ½-inch-thick lines) drawn on an 8.5-by-11-inch piece of colored paper (use a calming color such as beige, pale yellow, blue, or green), laminated if possible

Directions:

1. Invite the child to sit in a comfortable position (cross-legged on the floor or sitting upright in a chair).

2. Welcome the child. Explain that this is a time to relax and focus on their breathing. Discuss how their body feels. Help them scan their body, instructing them to notice how their head, eyes, shoulders, belly, legs, toes, and feet feel.

3. Hand the child the rectangle. Ask the child to trace the shape with their finger. Have the child count to four while they trace the short side and count to 6 while they trace the longer side. Have them trace the entire figure at least twice, counting as they go.

CONTINUED

4. Now, add breathing to the tracing. Instead of having the child count out loud, have them inhale for 4 counts on the short sides. Encourage the child to breathe in through their nose. Then have them breathe out for 6 counts on the longer sides. Repeat three times.

5. Encourage the child to continue breathing in this pattern, removing the need to trace with the finger. Invite the child to close their eyes and repeat the pattern for 3 more cycles.

6. Congratulate the child at the end. Discuss how their body feels now. Help them scan their body, noticing how their head, eyes, shoulders, belly, legs, toes, and feet feel.

Flying Saucer Ride

Children love to go on an adventure. This activity takes the child on an adventure meditation into their inner awareness. Often children who are sensory over-responsive need assistance to examine who they are and how they feel. Remember that it's easier to relax in a quiet space with dimmed lighting. This activity may be especially helpful before stressful events.

ACTIVITY TYPE: Mindfulness

What You'll Need:

- Quiet room free of distractions (no TV or distracting noises in the background)
- Comfortable mat or couch
- Weighted blanket or light sheet
- Soft cloth (optional)

Directions:

1. Encourage the child to lie on their back and cover themselves with a light sheet or weighted blanket. Invite them to close their eyes or cover their eyes with a soft cloth.

2. Once they are settled, read the following script, speaking slowly and softly:

   Imagine a warm summer evening. You are walking in the backyard through thick, green grass. The birds are singing. [Pause.] The air feels cool and clean as you breathe in through your nose and out through your mouth. Breathe in again through your nose and out through your mouth.

   The sky is clear tonight, with stars shining brightly. In the sky, you notice a soft shimmering light. It appears to be moving toward you.

   Focus your attention on your heart. Imagine there is a warm, golden light. As you breathe into your heart, the warm, golden light fills you with love. Feel the warm, loving glow as it flows slowly down your arms, softly spilling into your hands until it spreads to your fingertips. Can you feel your heart grow warmer and bigger? [Pause.]

CONTINUED

The glowing light gets closer. You notice it looks like a disc. It looks silvery now, as it flies closer and finally lands not far from where you're standing.

You see me come out of the flying saucer, and I invite you to join me inside. You are filled with feelings of safety and love as I invite you to walk up the steps.

Put your hands on the saucer and notice how it feels. Is it warm or cold? Hard, sleek, smooth? I invite you to come inside with me. Before you enter, you notice a box near the door with the words, "Worry Box." This box accepts anything you would like to put inside. [Pause.] Imagine putting your worries inside that box.

The flying saucer is ready for takeoff now. Take a seat. Notice how you feel. [Pause.] As the saucer takes off, feel the breeze on your body. Together, you and I enjoy the view above the house. Relax and enjoy the ride. [Pause.]

Listen for sounds. What do you hear? Notice any smells. What does it feel like where you are? [Pause.]

Now it's time to return home. Slowly, the flying saucer goes back down, back home. Relax and enjoy the ride.

When the flying saucer lands, step off. You are back where you started. Notice how peaceful it feels. Perhaps your heart is filled with peace and gratitude as well. [Pause.]

If your eyes are closed, open them whenever you are ready. You may notice that you feel fully alert but also very relaxed.

3. Take a moment to have the child describe their visit—what they saw, heard, and smelled—while in the flying saucer.

VARIATION: You can adapt this script to your child's interests. Perhaps they want to go for a ride on a magic carpet, a horse and buggy, or a hot-air balloon. Also, if you don't have a grassy backyard, you can have them envision a local park. Make whatever modifications you need to help your child visualize the scene.

One Minute of Peace

This quick guided meditation can help your child calm and center themselves before hurrying on to their next activity.

ACTIVITY TYPE: **Mindfulness**

What You'll Need:

- Quiet room free of distractions (no TV or distracting noises in the background)

- Comfortable mat or couch

- Weighted blanket or light sheet

- Soft cloth (optional)

Directions:

1. Encourage the child to lie on their back and cover themselves with a light sheet or weighted blanket. Invite them to close their eyes or cover their eyes with a soft cloth.

2. Once they are settled, read the following script, speaking slowly and softly:

   Inhale deeply. Feel your tummy and chest rise. Slowly exhale and let all the air leave your lungs. [Pause.] Keep focusing on your breath, inhale and exhale.

   Every time you breathe in, feel your tummy and chest rise. Every time you breathe out, feel your tummy and chest relax.

   Feel all your muscles in your legs and arms relax. Feel the tension in your body release. Listen to your breath. [Pause.]

   Relax your mind. Let go of all your worries and concerns. See them float away. Inhale. Exhale. [Pause.]

   Open your heart and let in love and comfort.

   Allow yourself one minute of feeling at absolute peace. [Pause for 1 minute.]

   When you are ready, open or uncover your eyes. Wiggle your fingers and toes. Slowly sit up, feeling fully alert and relaxed.

The Infinity Walk Plus

The Infinity Walk (page 40) is a good therapeutic method for progressively developing coordination. This variation of the earlier activity is for a child who is able to do the Infinity Walk without tripping or losing eye contact.

ACTIVITY TYPE: Proprioception, Vestibular, Visual tracking

What You'll Need:

- A prepared Infinity Walk course (see page 40 for setup)

- A 2-by-3-foot sign with letters large enough to see from 10 feet away (You can write anything you'd like on the sign, such as an inspirational or important message.)

Directions:

1. Position yourself to the right of the intersecting lines, about 4 feet away. While the child is walking the course, hold up the sign. Have the child read the letters of the sign out loud. It is not important for them to read the words; you just want them to focus on the letters.

2. After a few rounds, instruct them to walk in the opposite direction, again reading the letters aloud.

VARIATIONS: There are many ways to vary the Infinity Walk Plus. Here are a few ways to make the walk more challenging for older children and to include a child who doesn't read yet:

- Have the child walk forward, then backward, and then sideways around the course.

- Have the child read words from the sign.

- Have the child read the letters backward (for example, if the sign says, "I love lunchtime," the child reads "e-m-i-t-h-c-n-u-l-l e-v-o-l-i."

- Children who don't read yet can identify animals, shapes, or colors on a sign.

- Play music and have the child march to the beat.

- Have the child play a musical instrument (tambourine, wooden sticks, or bells) to the beat of their marching.

Playing with Dogs

This activity is an adaptation of several yoga poses I use with children in my clinic. (I've included the Sanskrit names you might hear in a yoga class, but the dog-related names are more fun.) This is not an activity involving a real dog. Rather, it allows the child to pretend to be a dog. The weight-bearing on all four limbs provides feedback about where the child's body is in space and stretches out the entire body. Playful noises help integrate all movements. Be silly and creative.

ACTIVITY TYPE: Mindfulness, Proprioception

What You'll Need:

- Clear, open space (such as a yard, gym, or carpeted room)

- Yoga mat

- Comfortable stretchy clothing

- Pictures of each pose (if possible) or demonstrate

Directions:

1. Familiarize the child with the following poses and instruct throughout the sequence:

   Downward Dog (Adho Mukha Svanasana) starts by standing upright with the feet shoulder-distance apart. Bring your arms up overhead, then bend at the waist and let your arms float down in a swan dive. Place your hands on the ground and walk them out in front of you. The end shape is an inverted V with your palms on the floor facing away, and toes (heels if flexible enough) on the ground. Stay in this position for 3 to 5 breaths, adjusting the hips to be more comfortable.

   Three-Legged Dog (Eka Pada Adho Mukha Svanasana) is a fun transition out of the Downward Dog. This pose starts in the Downward Dog position. Raise the right foot up to the ceiling. Point the toe to the ceiling, keeping the hips straight.

CONTINUED

Upward Dog (Urdhva Mukha Svanasana) is the reverse of Downward Dog. From Downward Dog, move into a flat plank position. Allow the hips to sink to the ground and the chest to raise. Flip your toes onto the ground. (This pose strengthens the vertebral column, wrists, and arms, while stretching the thorax, abdomen, lungs, and shoulders.)

Child's Pose (Balasana) is essentially curling up in a ball on the floor. Kneel on the mat with your knees separated and lower the torso between the knees. Lean forward and put the top of the head on the ground, with arms resting alongside the body.

2. Begin the sequence standing up straight and tall like a mountain.

3. Move into the Downward Dog position. From here, lift up the right leg into Upward Dog. Breathe in and out. Bark! Breathe again.

4. Return the right foot to the ground, and then gently bring your hips to the ground. Flip your toes so they rest on the ground and lift up the chest into the Upward Dog position. Breathe and bark!

5. When you are ready to rest, shift the hips back toward the feet, to Child's Pose. Stay in this position for 3 to 5 breaths.

6. Repeat the sequence, lifting the left leg instead of the right.

Crazy Dogs

Crazy Dogs involves more complex dog positions than Playing with Dogs. It takes more coordination and practice to master. Crossing the midline while upside down helps the over-responsive child integrate both sides of their brain. The weight-bearing on all four limbs provides feedback about where the child's body is in space and stretches out the entire body, while playful noises help integrate all movements. Be silly and creative.

ACTIVITY TYPE: Mindfulness, Proprioception

What You'll Need:

- Clear, open space (such as a yard, gym, or carpeted room)

- Yoga mat

- Comfortable stretchy clothing

- Pictures of each pose (if possible) or demonstrate

Directions:

1. Familiarize the child with the following poses and instruct throughout the sequence:

   Dog Twist: From the Downward Dog position (see page 53), lift the right arm. Bring it toward the left leg in a gentle twist. Bring the right arm up to the left knee or ankle. If possible, hold the left ankle with the right hand.

   Fire Hydrant Dog (Open Dog): From Three-Legged Dog (see page 53), lift the right leg. Open the hips toward the right side and bend the knee. Of course, when a dog lifts his leg, he is marking his territory. (Children often giggle about this dog position.)

CONTINUED

Puppy Pose (Uttana Shishosana): From Child's Pose (see page 54), raise up the hips so that the legs are 90 degrees to the ground. At the same time, extend your arms in front of your head. This stretch feels especially good across the shoulders. The chin or forehead can rest on the ground, depending on the child's flexibility.

2. Follow the sequence in Playing with Dogs (see page 53), but now incorporate the additional poses as indicated.

TIP: Be sure to make the practice fun by incorporating sounds. A dog can yelp, bark, and snarl, loudly and softly. A dog can also pant, lick their lips, and even smile. Connect each dog sound with a specific movement, and the child will be giggling and trying to stretch even farther.

Too Little! Too Much!

This activity teaches children to self-judge what is too much, too little, and just right, building insight and giving the child control over what they want.

ACTIVITY TYPE: Auditory, Olfactory, Tactile, Vestibular

What You'll Need:

- Music and a speaker

- Various scents, including peppermint, vanilla, and something smelly (such as an onion, musk, dirty sock, or rag)

- Sit 'n' Spin or other rotating toy

Directions:

1. Introduce the game by sharing that there are times when you like a lot of sensory input and others when you get too much. Explain to the child that they will be practicing identifying what is too little, too much, and just right.

2. Start with the auditory sense, as volume is easily understood. Play a song at a very low volume. Ask the child, "Is this too much or too little?" Say, "If it's too much, put your hands over your ears. If too little, ask for the volume to be raised. If it's just right, make the OK sign." Have the child practice this until they understand the concept. Using the same process, expose the child to the various smells, starting with peppermint. Have them identify if it's too little, too much, or just right. Expose child to the vanilla scent. Then expose them to something that is smelly. If too much, have the child pinch their nose and back away. If too little, have the child lean forward. If just right, have the child make the OK sign.

3. Now have child get on the Sit 'n' Spin. Rotate them 5 times. If too much, have them act dizzy. If too little, have them ask for more. If just right, have them make the OK sign.

VARIATION: The child can also use flash cards to tell you if something is too much, too little, or just right. For example, on a green card, write, "Just Right." On a red card, write, "Too Much." And on a blue card, write, "Too Little." This variation on the game gives the child visual input to help reinforce the concept. Really, any three colors can be used, but green, red, and blue align with the colors used in the Zones of Regulation curriculum.

Ball Massage

Something wonderful happens when a child receives a massage. There's a general sense of calming and relaxation. This activity uses gentle acupressure to release tightness. It can be done by a trusted adult or you can teach your child how to do self-massage. Children who are eight years and older may be able to massage themselves. Model for your child how to do the massage pattern initially, and then allow them to try this activity at the same time as you massage your own feet. This massage is done with shoes off and socks on.

ACTIVITY TYPE: Proprioception, Tactile

What You'll Need:
- A variety of clean balls, less than 4 inches in diameter (see Alternative Equipment on page 59).
- A mat

Directions:
1. Have the child choose their favorite type of ball.
2. Start by sitting down on the mat with the child. Place the child's feet flat on the mat so that their knees are bent.
3. Place the ball under the child's right foot, starting up by the toes. Using firm pressure to hold the foot, massage the child's toes slowly one at a time with the ball. Press each toe individually, holding at each toe for at least 30 seconds.
4. Next, move the ball up to the ball of the child's right foot. Press it into the fleshy part of the foot at the base of the toes. Ask the child if there are tender spots. If the child identifies tenderness, move slowly and carefully, noticing how it feels to press hard and soft.
5. Move the ball to the middle area of the child's foot. Here the child can wiggle their foot in circular patterns, moving from right to left and up and down. This should feel good, especially in the inner sole. Ask the child how much or how little pressure they prefer.
6. Move to the heel now. Here the child should tolerate almost full pressure on the ball.

7. Ask the child to breathe in, hold it, breathe out, and rest. *[Pause.]*

8. Now wiggle the ball up toward the calf of the child's right leg. Again, ask the child to breathe in, hold it, breathe out, and rest. *[Pause.]*

9. Wiggle the ball in circles along the calf muscle. Ask the child to tell you if there are tender parts. Just let the ball rest on those parts, gently rolling the ball around the tender areas. Ask the child to breathe in, hold it, breathe out, and rest. *[Pause.]*

10. Repeat steps 3 to 9 for the left side. It's important to massage both sides of the body equally.

TIP: Work slowly, being sure to remind the child to breathe in, hold it, breathe out, and rest before you begin each new step. Be sure to use a lot of pressure with the ball.

ALTERNATIVE EQUIPMENT: You can also use tennis balls or racquetballs. Each ball has a different texture and will give a different type of feeling. Be sure these balls are new and clean.

Jamari: Tactile Defensiveness

Eight-year-old Jamari just started third grade. He is an extremely picky eater, which makes eating at school very hard. He only eats white foods (bread, potatoes, and popcorn) and crunchy and salty foods (chips and pretzels), and he avoids all vegetables and most meats. He will occasionally eat a chicken nugget, but only if it's from a specific box.

Jamari's parents took him to a pediatric occupational therapist, who completed a comprehensive sensory processing assessment. The therapist shared that Jamari is sensory over-responsive. He has characteristics of tactile defensiveness, which means he is overly sensitive to tactile input. This makes playing in messy environments difficult and eating foods with textures even harder. The therapist set up a clinic program that included sensory-stimulating activities. Initially, Jamari resisted getting messy. As part of the home program, Jamari's parents exposed him to messy activities, including finger painting, playing in a rice bin, and drawing with shaving cream.

His parents also started playing ball massage on his feet. Initially, Jamari was very tickly and hesitant to have his feet touched. When he was in control of the ball, he began to relax and enjoy the feeling. He noticed his feet tingling and liked how his feet felt afterward.

Six months later, Jamari's therapist began working on his picky eating habits. He is learning good nutrition principles and experimenting with putting fruits onto a spoon. He has not yet tried vegetables, but he's curious about smoothies.

CHAPTER FIVE

Activities for Sensory Under-Responsiveness

Children who are sensory under-responsive are often quiet and passive, and disregard stimuli available in their environment. These children take longer to register a sensory event. Their under-responsivity may lead to poor body awareness, clumsiness, or awkward movements. These children are often accident-prone and fall when they aren't paying full attention to where they are walking. They need more input to self-regulate. They may do better in a more spontaneous and chaotic environment.

Activities for children who display characteristics of sensory under-responsiveness focus on intensity of sensory input. These children may have difficulty figuring out what they need to do or when they need to stop, and they may want simpler activities with basic start and stop directions. Activities with lots of movement and heavy work provide more grounding and calming effects. They also need more input to get their under-responsive nervous systems engaged. I often let the child practice first and then invite their siblings to join in the activities to involve the whole family. If you have other children, you may want to do the same.

Oral Sorting

The mouth provides abundant sensory input to the body. Sucking and blowing help with calming and organization. This game is an easy one to set up. Use brightly colored plates, cups, and straws to add visual input.

ACTIVITY TYPE: Oral motor, Total body strength

SAFETY TIPS: Not recommended for children under age 3 as the straws can be a choking hazard. Sequins *must* be wider than the straw openings. Use a new straw for each player for safety and hygiene.

What You'll Need:
- Scissors
- Glue
- 6 paper cups in 6 different colors
- 1 strong paper plate
- A handful of large round sequins (at least ¾-inch in diameter) in colors that match each cup
- Several straws of varying length and diameter

Directions:
1. Cut the paper cups in half around the diameter, approximately halfway through the height of the cup. Glue the bottom of the cups to the plate. Wait for them to dry.
2. Place the cup-lined plate within reach of the child. Scatter the sequins around the plate. Set the straws to the side for the child to choose from.
3. Let the child choose a straw and put one end in their mouth.
4. Have the child suck on the straw to create enough suction to pick up a sequin with the end of the straw. (Larger straws are easier to suck but less specific on the direction of sucking. Smaller straws are harder to suck, but it's easier to pick up the small sequins.)
5. Have the child continue to suck in and move the sequin over to the matching-color cup and then drop it in. Continue the game until all the items are in the cups.

Matthew: Everything Goes in His Mouth

Marge is the mother of three-year-old Matthew—a darling, active boy. Matthew has not yet begun preschool. His parents are concerned because he puts everything in his mouth, which can be dangerous. In fact, they just returned from the emergency room because Matthew swallowed a LEGO piece. This was their third trip this year to the ER. Matthew also eats everything he can get his hands on, especially if it's crunchy, salty, or sweet. As a result, Matthew weighs 45 pounds (an average weight for a three-year-old boy is 31.5 pounds).

Marge and her spouse are very worried about Matthew's safety, as well as his weight, especially since obesity runs in Marge's family. Their family doctor recommended they consult a dietician and an occupational therapist. Following the therapist's assessment, Mathew was found to be sensory under-responsive, especially in his mouth. The therapist recommended a home program to help Matthew inhibit the need for everything to go into his mouth. This included oral massage, which involves a massage of the scalp, face, and jaw, as well as a straw-use program to strengthen his mouth muscles. Matthew began using a straw when drinking, starting with very small straws when drinking clear liquids. This progressed to larger straws with thickened liquids. Matthew also learned how to sort colored items using a straw in the "Oral Sorting" game.

In addition, Marge purchased some inexpensive mouth toys, including bubbles and whistles. Matthew's favorite was a Chewy Tube (an oral motor tube), which he could just leave in his mouth and crunch on. Instead of always putting food in his mouth, he learned to get soothing and heavy work in his mouth with non-food items.

The Sloth

This activity challenges the child to hold on to a horizontal bolster swing as it sways, much the same way a sloth would hold on to a thick branch with all its limbs. Children who are sensory under-responsive really enjoy the challenge of holding on to the swing with their full body.

ACTIVITY TYPE: Core and upper-body strength, Proprioception, Vestibular

SAFETY TIPS: Play this game on a soft surface and have lots of padding underneath for safety. The child should weigh 100 pounds or less, depending on the equipment.

What You'll Need:

- A horizontal glider bolster swing or similar (see DIY Tip below)

- Crash pad, mat, or pillows

Directions:

1. Have the child lie on their stomach on the bolster, holding on with arms and legs.

2. Over the crash pad, mat, or pillows, swing the bolster either forward and backward or from side to side in a gentle, rhythmic motion. Instruct the child to hold on tight with both their arms and legs.

3. As the child gets comfortable with the swinging, you may guide the bolster to turn over, leaving the child hanging upside down. Challenge the child to stay on as long as possible. You can even challenge your child to time how long they stay on.

TIP: This activity is especially good for under-responsive children, but sensory seekers enjoy the intensity and gentle competition as well.

VARIATION: The child can ride the swing sitting up and holding both ropes, or side straddle, holding on to one side. To make this game even more exciting, change the "Sloth" into a "Hurricane" by trying to swing the child off in a fun manner with lots of giggles and gentle competition. (The child can try to beat their time staying on.) It's a super-fun variation and gets kids to use all of their muscles trying to hang on. Always remember to keep a mat or crash pad underneath to support them if and when they drop.

DIY TIP: Don't have a horizontal bolster? You can create a makeshift bolster with a 2-by-6-foot plank, a heavy blanket, and some duct tape. Wrap the blanket around the board for cushioning and secure with duct tape. This requires 2 strong adults to hold on to the ends of the board, but it can be just as fun.

Tractor Pull

This activity is similar to the Human Sling (see page 31) but instead of picking up the child in the sheet, you pull the sheet across the floor. The added input from being dragged across the floor is a fun way for the child to get extra heavy work.

ACTIVITY TYPE: Core strength, Heavy work, Vestibular

SAFETY TIP: This is best if the child weighs less than 75 pounds but depends on the strength of the adults.

What You'll Need:

- Floor with mats or a smooth floor

- An old, clean sheet

- Pillows and/or cushions (optional)

- Plastic fruits and vegetables (optional)

- Two strong adults

Directions:

1. Spread out the sheet, and if using, place a few pillows and/or cushions along the path you'll be taking. You can also place the fruits and vegetables in random places for the child to grab as their "tractor" goes by.

2. Ask the child to pick a verbal command they can use to stop once things get started, and then invite the child to lie on their back in the middle of the sheet.

3. Each adult picks up the 2 corners of the sheet on their side and drags the sheet and child forward.

4. You can have the child pick up the plastic vegetables and fruit along the way, pretending to be a farmer picking their crops. You can also drag them over the "bumps in the road" (pillows and cushions).

5. If the child indicates that the activity should be stopped (or when the game naturally concludes), drop the ends of the sheet and allow the child to climb off.

TIP: After being dragged, the child can trade places with one of the adults for more input. Having the child pull the sheet along provides lots of heavy work.

Helicopter Ride

The swinging circles in this game can be gentle or fast, depending on the child's needs. Because they are self-propelling, the child is in control. This can be particularly fun and stimulating because you can change the texture of the swing by using carpet squares, soft surfaces, or a harder/coarse surface to cover the platform.

ACTIVITY TYPE: Proprioception, Upper-body strength, Vestibular, Visual tracking

SAFETY TIP: Do not have the child on a swing for longer than five minutes. Children become easily overstimulated as a result of too much vestibular input. Be sure to rest in between turns, and then return to the game.

What You'll Need:
- A horizontal platform swing with a rotational device (see Alternative Equipment below)

Directions:
1. Have the child lie on the swing with their arms and head off the swing.

2. Invite the child to self-propel by making circles with their arms, being sure the arms cross over each other to promote crossing midline.

3. The child goes in circles until they are going fast enough and then stops pushing. They then fly like a helicopter around and around until the swing stops.

TIP: Crossing the midline of one's body means to spontaneously reach from one side to the other without planning or thought. Being able to cross midline allows us to fully interact with the environment. If one hand is busy, the other one can reach across and grab what is needed. The ability to cross midline also means that both sides of the brain integrate and work together.

ALTERNATIVE EQUIPMENT: Don't have a horizontal platform swing? Use a scooter board instead. Otherwise, you can use a low stool, Sit 'n' Spin, wobble chair, or an armless and backless computer chair in the lowest position. The child can lie over it, hold up their head, arms, legs, and propel themselves in circles as described.

VARIATION: Have the child swing forward and backward, from side to side, in circles (spin to carve out a circle), and in rotation (spins on axis).

Spinning Cyclone

This activity provides movement forward and backward, from side to side, axial rotation (spins on axis), and circular rotation (spins to carve out a circle). It is especially attractive to children who are sensory under-responsive as well as sensory seeking. This is a good outdoor activity when the weather is nice. Many local parks have a tire swing.

ACTIVITY TYPE: Proprioception, Vestibular, Visual tracking

SAFETY TIP: Do not have the child on a swing for longer than five minutes. Children become easily overstimulated as a result of receiving too much vestibular input. Be sure to rest in between turns, and then return to the game.

What You'll Need:
- Tire swing, hanging either vertically or horizontally (see Alternative Equipment below)

Directions:
1. Have your child sit on the swing (sitting upright with feet in middle or inside the saddle depending on the tire's orientation).

2. Start swinging the child in a circular motion. Push slowly and steadily until child grows used to the movement.

3. Increase the swinging motion, making it go faster and faster, to create a "cyclone." The child's request to stop should be honored.

TIP: Tire swings are often found at public playgrounds. While you can purchase one, some families choose to make them out of recycled tires or inner tubes. These swings can be sat in, stood up on safely, and ridden like a horse if it is vertical (one leg on either side).

ALTERNATIVE EQUIPMENT: If you can't find a tire swing, you can use an armless/backless computer chair in its lowest position or a Sit 'n' Spin.

Shape Changer

This activity uses a body sock made from Lycra, and when the child wears it, they essentially become a "shape changer." Lycra provides resistance on every plane, making it extra challenging to move around.

ACTIVITY TYPE: Heavy work, Proprioceptive, Total body strength

SAFETY TIP: Do this activity on a soft surface for protection against falls.

What You'll Need:

- Commercial Lycra body sock or DIY (see page 72) appropriate for your child's size

- Soft surface and plenty of space to move around

Directions:

1. Hold up the body sock so that corners are high and low, making a rectangle shape. Invite the child step in with feet first. Instruct them to place their feet in the lower corners and their arms in the upper corners.

2. Close up the Velcro opening if the child is okay with putting their head inside. Otherwise, it's fine for their head to stick out the opening. (It's still fun that way.)

3. Have your child move around in the body sock, shifting their shape. They can start in a crouched position and then stand up and stretch. They can roll on mats, walk forward and backward, and jump up and down. The options for movement are limited only by your and your child's imaginations.

Activities for Sensory Under-Responsiveness   **71**

Making Your Own Lycra Sensory Tools

Lycra is a brand name for a highly elastic synthetic fabric, which bathing suits are often made from. This material provides endless possibilities for sensory input. Most of the Lycra items I mention in the activities throughout this part of the book can be purchased, but if you're crafty and you have a serger (a specialized sewing machine), you can make them yourself.

It's a good idea to purchase the material from a fabric store in the fall and winter seasons when it's typically on sale. When creating a Lycra tool, measure it to the size of your child and then make it smaller, so that it compresses. It is best to use a pattern, which you can find online, but here are a few recommended measurements:

To make a tunnel: Measure it two to three inches smaller than the basic girth of your child.

To make a compression loop: Measure one-half to two-thirds the size of your child's height.

To make a body sock: Measure five to six inches shorter than your child's height.

Wristband Chewy

Under-responsive children often seek out oral input. They need more input in their mouths and may overstuff their mouths when eating. They may also chew on nonfood items like their clothes (for example, shirt collars or sleeves), which can be distressing to parents. This activity helps you provide your child with a piece of clothing that's okay to chew on. It's also easy to wash.

ACTIVITY TYPE: Gustatory, Oral motor, Proprioception

What You'll Need:

- Colorful wristbands made from terry cloth or DIY (see DIY Tip on page 74)

- One adult-size wristband

- Flavored food-grade extracts such as peppermint, vanilla, and/or almond

Directions:

1. Show the wristbands to the child. Explain that this is clothing that can be put in their mouth, as opposed to their other clothing like jackets, collars, and shirt sleeves.

2. Have the child choose a flavored food-grade extract by placing a drop onto their hand and testing it out. If they like it, dab one of the wristbands with the flavoring. Do the same with your adult wristband.

CONTINUED

3. Place the flavored band on the child's wrist or let them put it on. Put yours on as well.

4. Together, practice chewing on your wristbands. This may feel awkward to you, but doing it along with the child normalizes it. As you practice, stress the point that the wristbands are okay to put in your mouth, but it's not okay to chew on other clothing.

5. Wash the bands regularly (a lingerie bag is helpful here to keep them from getting "lost" in the washer or dryer). Provide the child with a fresh wristband chewy each day.

TIP: A wristband chewy is a good item to include in the Sensory Box (see page 102).

DIY TIP: If you cannot find wrist sweatbands appropriately sized for your child, you can make your own. Purchase stretchy terry cloth in at least three different colors in 1-by-1-foot dimensions. Measure the diameter of your child's wrist. Using pinking shears to avoid fraying the fabric, cut the terry cloth a half-inch smaller by 1 inch. (For example, if your child's wrist is 4 inches in diameter, cut out the terry cloth to 3.5 by 1 inch.) Fold in half lengthwise and sew along the seam to form a tube that can be slipped onto the wrist. Finish off the edges to avoid fraying. (If you use a sewing machine, the band will likely last longer.)

Circle Peekaboo!

This game gets the child used to spinning and paying attention to a fixed spot. The spinning helps them improve their vestibular ability. While a computer chair is used in this activity, a mesh net swing, Sit 'n' Spin, or even a tire swing at the park can work just as well.

ACTIVITY TYPE: Deep pressure, Heavy work, Vestibular, Visual tracking

What You'll Need:

- An armless and backless computer chair

- Various objects

Directions:

1. Invite the child to sit upright or lie on their stomach on the chair.

2. Spin the child around to the right side first. The child can also self-propel by kicking with their feet or pushing with their arms. Next, spin to the left. Be sure to rotate in both directions.

3. To add visual tracking to the spinning, play peekaboo with various objects. Each time the child rotates around, they will look at the object you are holding and identify it. For example, you hold up a stuffed bear, and the child says, "I see a bear," or you hold up a pencil, and the child says, "I see a pencil."

4. Depending on the child's tolerance for movement, continue this game for up to 1 minute in each direction.

VARIATIONS: You can have the child read a letter/word on a printed card, identify how many fingers you are holding up, or look at math flash cards and solve an equation.

Camila: Accident-Prone

Nine-year-old Camila is in third grade. She's very clumsy, which her mom thought was due to her being overweight. She broke both arms in a two-month period from tripping and while riding her bike. The doctor said the breaks were not due to a medical problem such as osteoporosis.

Following an occupational therapist's assessment for coordination and balance, Camila was found to be sensory under-responsive. Her therapist recommended lots of heavy work and vestibular input. Her home program recommended she play outside as much as possible, running, riding her bike, and playing on the monkey bars. Her parents supervised while she played on the jungle gym and her bike. They also found a Sit 'n' Spin toy at a local garage sale. Camila used the Sit 'n' Spin three times every day. At first, she said she was very dizzy and had to sit down. Over time, Camila didn't feel as dizzy and tolerated the rotational movement easier.

Camila also began a new game called "Circle Peekaboo" to improve her visual tracking and vestibular sense. Her parents held up math flash cards while she moved in circles on a computer chair. On the first rotation she looked at the card and on the next rotation she answered the math problem. Every second rotation, her parents held up a new card. In these ways, Camila improved her ability to balance and is not nearly as clumsy around the playground. She hasn't broken any more bones recently, and she is working on a weight-loss and nutritious eating program.

Surfing on Land

This activity requires a good imagination because the child will pretend to be surfing in the ocean while listening to "beach" music. In reality, they'll be on a surfboard (real or makeshift) on a soft surface. This game can be played outdoors on the grass or indoors on a mat.

ACTIVITY TYPE: Auditory, Motor planning, Proprioception, Vestibular

What You'll Need:

- Painted cardboard surfboard or real surfboard (or see Alternative Equipment on page 78)

- Soft indoor or outdoor surface

- Music: "Surfin' in My Imagination" by Ralph's World (available on YouTube)

Directions:

1. Place the surfboard on a soft surface.

2. Have your child begin by lying on the surfboard. Let them know a big wave is coming and instruct them to stand up so they can surf the wave. To keep their balance in the "water," they should practice bending their knees and pumping slightly, standing sideways, and alternate standing on 1 foot and then the other.

3. Shout, "Wipe out!" and the child can practice falling into the "water" (onto the mat or ground) safely.

CONTINUED

4. Once the child gets these movements down, listen to the song "Surfin' in My Imagination." Have the child listen closely to the song. You can also listen beforehand so the child knows what to expect.

5. When the song says, "Surfing in my imagination," the child will pretend to surf the way they practiced, keeping their balance in the "water." When the song says, "Stand on one foot," the child lifts one of their feet. When the song says, "Wipe out," the child "falls" off the board onto the soft surface.

TIP: You can use other beach music like "Surfin' Safari" by the Beach Boys (also available on YouTube), but because the lyrics won't correspond to the movements, the child will need to rely more on their imagination.

ALTERNATIVE EQUIPMENT: You can use a BOSU ball or balance board for this activity, which will be a little more difficult. You can also use a skateboard with the wheels removed or even a piece of plywood for the surfboard.

Cotton Ball Keep-Away

This blowing game, which can be played indoors or outdoors, is not only fun but can also be very calming to the under-responsive child.

ACTIVITY TYPE: Oral motor

SAFETY TIP: All participants should be free of colds and other contagious illnesses.

What You'll Need:

- 2 to 4 participants
- A clean twin sheet or large pillowcase
- A thick cotton ball

Directions:

1. Each participant holds a side of the sheet, bringing it up to their face and stepping back until the sheet is taut. If adults are playing, they should kneel to the height of the child.

2. Place 1 cotton ball on the stretched-out sheet.

3. Someone says, "Go," and the participants start blowing to keep the cotton ball away from their side of the sheet. If the cotton ball gets blown off near someone's side of the sheet, just pick it up and try again.

TIP: The size of the sheet or pillowcase you use depends on how many participants are playing. A queen-size sheet, for instance, would work for 4 to 6 players, while a pillowcase would be good for just 2.

Scooter Board "Rowing"

This scooter board race involves having the child sit upright on the board, grasp a plunger in both hands, and propel themselves forward. Balance and concentration are needed to coordinate using the plunger to move forward. This activity is easier to do outside on smooth concrete or playground surface. Otherwise, play it in an indoor hallway or gym surface that is clean and clear of obstacles.

ACTIVITY TYPE: Proprioception, Total body strength, Vestibular

SAFETY TIP: Child should wear a safety helmet and gloves for protection.

What You'll Need:

- Scooter board
- New toilet plunger
- Chalk or painter's tape

Directions:

1. Have the child sit upright in a crisscross position on the scooter board.

2. The child grasps the plunger and practices using it as an oar to propel forward.

3. You can time the child as they propel forward and reach the finish line you establish using chalk or painter's tape.

VARIATIONS: Make this activity a fun competition by having more than one participant follow a path to the finish line, or add another layer of competition by timing the race and seeing if participants can improve their timing.

DIY TIP: You can make your own scooter board from a flat plastic or wood surface with 4 caster wheels firmly affixed to the 4 bottom corners.

Scooter Board Obstacle Course

Obstacle courses are a wonderful tool in all parts of children's play. In this activity, the child must go through an obstacle course while lying on their tummy. The heavy work of self-propelling with their hands and arms is calming and helps a child with sensory under-responsiveness focus and transition between tasks.

ACTIVITY TYPE: Core strength, Motor planning, Proprioception, Vestibular

SAFETY TIP: Child should wear a safety helmet and gloves for protection.

What You'll Need:
- Smooth outdoor surface
- Chalk, painter's tape, and/or toy cones for marking the course
- Scooter board
- Stopwatch

Directions:
1. Set up the obstacle course to prepare for the game. I always start with a shorter version, using 2 to 3 steps. When a child masters the short course, increase the number of steps. This is a good activity to see how many steps your child can remember. Create the obstacle course in an open space (gym or playground). Put out cones to mark turns, and use chalk or painter's tape to indicate the finish. The course should be 20- to 30-feet long and include straight, zigzag, and curved lines. Start out simple, as this course is challenging for the upper body.

2. Review the obstacle course with the child, giving instructions to follow the taped lines in order.

3. Have the child lie on the scooter board on their tummy. On hearing, "Go," they should navigate along the path, propelling themselves with their body.

4. Time how long this takes. If successful, celebrate, and then add on another obstacle.

TIP: This game is also fun as a gentle competition. You can create obstacles by having the child go under chairs/tables, up a plank, and down a gentle ramp.

Mail Carrier

Children of all ages enjoy playing in tunnels. Younger children tend to enjoy easy pop-up Lycra tunnels with smaller diameters (one to two feet in diameter) and solid sides. Older children ages five to ten still enjoy this size tunnel but may have to belly crawl through.

ACTIVITY TYPE: Heavy work, Proprioceptive, Total body strength

What You'll Need:

- Commercial Lycra tunnel or DIY (see page 72)

Directions:

1. Set out the Lycra tunnel, with one adult on each end holding the tunnel to keep it steady as the child crawls through.

2. Give your child a message to deliver from you on one end to the adult on the other end. It could be a math problem, a short message, or a question to answer.

3. The child kneels down and crawls through the tunnel—forward, backward, or on their belly. (Vary the method for each "delivery." For example, say, "Please deliver this message backward.")

VARIATIONS: A child who needs more input can also push a ball through the tunnel with their head. Start with a regular playground ball. Once this movement is mastered, you can increase to a medicine ball or another ball with more resistance. Another idea is to have them move a Ping-Pong ball through the tunnel by blowing at it through a straw. You can also add a little gentle competition by timing their passage through the tunnel.

Samar: Poor Proprioception

Samar is a seven-year-old boy with Down syndrome who has very poor proprioception. He attends second grade in a self-contained classroom. He has very low muscle tone and poor strength throughout his body. He often runs into walls while walking, trips over rocks, and drops his lunch tray in the cafeteria. He is overall sensory under-responsive and needs a lot of input to focus, learn, and live in his body.

Samar used to attend occupational and physical therapy but graduated when he learned to walk and run. After reading about proprioception, his parents tried a new approach. His mother is creative and has a serger (a type of sewing machine). She bought several yards of Lycra at the fabric store and sewed two tunnels. One was three feet in diameter and ten feet long, and the other one was two feet in diameter and fifteen feet long.

Samar started crawling through the ten-foot tunnel. He initially got stuck in the middle. His parents cheered him on to keep going. One parent looked in, playing peekaboo, and Samar giggled and crawled through. After a few weeks, he was ready to crawl through the fifteen-foot tunnel. His parents stretched it out in the living room. He smiled at the bright colors of the tunnel and belly crawled all the way through it.

These tunnels promoted proprioceptive input and deep pressure, which is important for body space awareness. Samar also started lifting weights with his father. Initially he could only lift two-pound weights but now he is lifting ten pounds. He now has a better sense of where his body is in space. His teachers report that he is tripping much less, doesn't run into walls, and can hold his cafeteria tray more easily.

Windmill

The Windmill is a simple activity that can be done inside or outside. The child may prefer to be on a soft mat in case they fall over. The Windmill requires the ability to cross midline on an unconscious level. This activity helps both sides of the brain integrate and work together.

ACTIVITY TYPE: Core strength, Motor planning, Proprioception, Vestibular

What You'll Need:

- Mat (optional)

Directions:

1. Start by having the child stand upright, with their legs shoulder-distance apart and arms outstretched.

2. Instruct the child to breathe in deeply, and on the exhale, cross their right hand to touch the left shin or foot (depending on flexibility). Have them hold for 5 seconds, and then stand up again. Now, instruct them to cross the left hand to touch the right shin or foot.

3. Repeat for 10 to 20 repetitions.

VARIATIONS: Vary this activity by changing the position of gravity: Try lying faceup on a mat or sitting on the mat with feet extended. You can also add hand weights to increase the work. You can instruct the child to touch their elbow to the opposite knee for a similar effect.

Soldier March

The Soldier March, which can be done indoors or outdoors, requires the ability to cross the midline of the body on an unconscious level. This activity helps both sides of the brain integrate and work together.

ACTIVITY TYPE: Core strength, Motor planning, Proprioception, Vestibular

What You'll Need:
- Mat (optional)

Directions:
1. Start by having the child stand upright with their legs shoulder-distance apart and arms extended straight out in front of the body. Instruct them to breathe in deeply.

2. On the exhale, have them lift the right leg straight up. At the same time, they should lift the right arm to above the head with the left arm remaining extended out in front. Have them hold for 3 to 5 seconds, and then release.

3. Breathe again, and on the exhale, have the child lift the left leg and arm straight up, and step forward.

4. Repeat the left-right pattern until the child starts marching in a coordinated manner. March 20 to 30 feet to get the rhythm down.

5. After a while, add music in the background so that the child can march to the beat.

6. Repeat for 10 to 20 repetitions.

VARIATIONS: This activity can be varied by changing the position of gravity. For example, it's possible to do this activity while lying on a mat, although there will obviously be no forward movement. This is a good adaptation if the child is having trouble with bilateral coordination. Another variation is to march by coordinating the different sides—that is, extend right arm and left leg, and then left arm and right leg. You can also add 1- to 2-pound wrist weights to increase the work.

Jumping Practice

Jumping on a trampoline helps children develop stronger muscles and better coordination. It also improves body-space, movement awareness, and balance, which help with walking and running. While the smaller trampoline in this activity can be used inside, if the weather is nice you can take it outdoors so your child can enjoy the weather. Children can jump for up to 30 minutes per day for maximum benefit. All children benefit from having a trampoline available to them.

ACTIVITY TYPE: Cardiovascular workout, Proprioception, Vestibular

SAFETY TIP: Always practice trampoline safety (see page 87).

What You'll Need:

- Three-foot trampoline (or larger)

Directions:

1. Have the child remove their shoes and climb onto the trampoline.

2. Let them get used to standing and bouncing a little on the trampoline.

3. Now, ask the child to jump up and down with their feet together and hands down by sides.

4. After a few minutes, call out different jumping styles, giving them a chance to practice each style for a few minutes: arms above head, jumping jacks, bunny hop, run to the end of the trampoline in each direction, etc.

5. The child can stay on the trampoline for up to 30 minutes, depending on their level of endurance.

VARIATION: Play red light/green light. When you say, "Green light," the child bounces and jumps on the trampoline. When you say, "Red light," the child freezes, which will be harder to do on the flexible surface.

Trampoline Benefits & Safety

Trampolines are one of my favorite tools for providing children with proprioceptive and vestibular input. They also build cardiovascular endurance; improve muscle tone, power, and endurance; promote restful sleep from the regular exercise; increase the child's visual awareness of their environment; and help the child build tolerance of movement. For all these reasons, I highly recommend purchasing a trampoline to give your child easy access to this wonderful sensory-stimulating tool. If you have the space and the funds, consider an outdoor in-ground trampoline, which is considered the safest. If not, a smaller trampoline is fine for the activities in this book.

With that said, trampolines *must* be used safely. Be sure to reference the trampoline's manual for safety information. The trampoline should conform to all safety standards. Using a trampoline safely will greatly reduce the chance of injuries. Be sure to follow these guidelines:

- Only one person on the trampoline at a time.

- Do not jump on a wet or dirty trampoline.

- An adult should be present for spotting or supervising the play.

- The child should only land on their feet or bottom, not other parts of the body.

- The child shouldn't attempt to flip or do other acrobatics that may result in landing incorrectly.

- Always use safety nets and pads.

- Springs should be covered with thick material to avoid catching fingers.

Trampoline-Style Simon Says

This is a variation of the classic game played on solid land. Playing Simon Says on a soft surface increases the balance and effort needed for the child to follow the instructions you call out. The larger the trampoline, the more creative you can be with the instructions.

ACTIVITY TYPE: Cardiovascular workout, Proprioception, Vestibular

SAFETY TIP: Always practice trampoline safety (see page 87).

What You'll Need:

- Three-foot trampoline (or larger)

Directions:

1. Have the child remove their shoes and climb onto the trampoline.

2. Let them get used to standing and bouncing a little on the trampoline.

3. Remind the child that they should only follow your instructions when you say "Simon says."

4. Some Simon Says instructions might be: jump once, jump twice, jump and clap once, jump and clap twice, hop on your right foot, hop on your left foot, shift to the right (or left), jump in a circle to the right (or left), sit, and jump. Use your imagination here, and don't forget to sometimes give the instruction without saying, "Simon says."

5. You can do this for as long as your child is enjoying it. After playing for a little while, they can just jump and play on the trampoline for up to 30 minutes.

Aluminum Foil Writing

This is a great activity to strengthen children's hand muscles and practice fine-motor activities using graded movement. Children with poor proprioception and hand strength sometimes use a "death grip" on their writing tool. This death grip causes hands to easily fatigue and makes writing cumbersome. Foil writing helps teach the child to grade appropriate pressure for gripping their pencil, retraining their hand muscles to loosen up. The goal is to write so that no lines or indents appear on the aluminum foil.

ACTIVITY TYPE: Fine motor, Proprioception, Upper-body and hand strength, Visual motor

What You'll Need:

- Pad of paper
- Heavy-duty aluminum foil
- Lined writing paper appropriate for the child's age
- Pencil

Directions:

1. Place a pad of paper directly on a table or desk and cover it with a flat piece of aluminum foil. Place a piece of lined paper over the foil.

2. Ask the child to copy or write a sentence appropriate for their age. First have the child write using maximum pressure on their pencil. Lift the paper and look together at the aluminum foil. What they wrote should clearly be reflected on the aluminum foil.

3. Next have them use less pressure. Check the aluminum foil to see if the words are reflected. If so, instruct the child to try using even less pressure.

4. Continue to practice, switching between heavy and light pressure, to train the child to use decreased pressure.

TIP: To further reinforce using less grip pressure, you can walk behind your child while they are sitting at the table and try stealing their pencil from their grip. If the child is holding on too tightly, you will not be able to take the pencil. This will help your child learn to lessen their pressure on the pencil.

Romper Stompers

This classic activity of walking on "stilts" is a source of endless fun, and an obstacle course makes it even more challenging.

ACTIVITY TYPE: Proprioception, Vestibular

SAFETY TIP: Don't do this activity barefoot. Wear sneakers for protection.

What You'll Need:

- A set of can stepper toys/walking cups (commercial or DIY; see DIY Tip below)

- A concrete surface or grassy lawn

- Chalk or painter's tape

- Obstacles, such as small toys (optional)

Directions:

1. While they hold both cords, have the child step up on one of the cans, and then step up on the second. Show them how to provide tension on the cords so that their feet are "glued" to the cans. Give the child time to gain their balance standing on the cans.

2. Spot the child as they pull on the cords and walk around on a concrete surface.

3. Once they can move around on the cans, you can create a short obstacle course by drawing a path with chalk or lining it out with painter's tape. Have the child carefully follow a line, perhaps going up a slight hill and down again, and walking over obstacles like a small toy. The possibilities for the obstacle course are limited only by your imagination.

DIY TIP: To make your own can stepper toys/walking cups, use two empty cans of equal size. For children age 7 and under, I recommend 29-ounce cans and for children age 7 and up, use 20-ounce cans. Have 2 strong cords that reach the length from your child's hands when their elbows are bent to the ground. Punch two holes in each can close to the edge of the bottom directly across from each other. String a cord through each can. Knot the cord inside the can using an overhand knot to make long handles.

Slingshot Scooter Board Ride

This is a good activity for core strengthening, as lying on the back with the head up is a challenging position. Be sure to offer breaks and keep an eye out for signs of fatigue.

ACTIVITY TYPE: Core strength, Proprioception, Vestibular

SAFETY TIP: Child should wear a safety helmet and gloves for protection.

What You'll Need:

- Scooter board
- 10 to 15 feet of strong rope
- Two adults per child
- Smooth playground, gym, or concrete surface
- Measuring tape

Directions:

1. Have the child lie on their back on the scooter board so that their back is firmly in the middle of the board, feet off one side and head on the other. The child must hold their head up so it doesn't touch the ground.

2. Two adults hold the rope while the child scoots around using their feet. Then have the child grab the rope with both hands.

3. Gently at first, the adults move the child around for practice and to get used to this position.

4. When ready, have the adults move the rope and child back and forth. Count to three. On the final count, the child lets go of the rope and is slung across the area. (In a small area, you may need to be sure any nearby walls are cushioned with mats in case the child hits the wall.)

5. Take a measurement of how far the child traveled each time, seeing if they can go farther on subsequent tries.

CHAPTER SIX

Activities for Sensory Seeking

A child who is sensory seeking actively seeks stimulation and may have an insatiable desire for sensory input. They tend to be constantly moving and will often crash and bump into things and people as they jump around. Children who are sensory seekers are very similar to sensory over-responders in that they seek out movement and touch input.

Calming activities for a sensory-seeking child focus on deep pressure and heavy work. This means that the activity involves applying heavy weight over the entire body. Heavy work is any type of activity that pulls or pushes against the body with resistance coming from weight in opposition to the body. There is resistance in the water while swimming, from weights when lifting, and when climbing on a jungle gym. The activities in this chapter feature tactile, proprioception, and vestibular input as calming forces.

Arms and Legs Animal Walks

Animal walks allow children to use their imagination and pretend that they are animals. Animal walks that require weight bearing on all four limbs are a wonderful way to improve strength in the shoulders and arms. The weight bearing on all four limbs promotes proprioception, calming, and relaxation. A favorite part of this activity is to imitate the animal noise, so don't forget to add the sounds that the animals make.

ACTIVITY TYPE: Cardiovascular workout, Deep pressure, Heavy work, Total body strength

Directions:

1. Do the bear walk. Have the child put their hands on the ground in front of their body a distance away, slightly bending knees as much as needed, while keeping their bottom high in the air. Instruct the child to step forward with their right hand and then their left foot. Next, have them step forward with the left arm and then their right foot. Repeat this action to progress forward. Encourage the child to growl.

2. Do the crab walk. Have the child lie on their back and use their hands and feet with knees bent to raise their trunk up. Prompt the child to imagine that their tummy is a flat table. Instruct the child to step forward by moving their right hand forward, followed by their left foot. Next move the left hand and then the right foot forward. Repeat this action to progress forward.

3. Do the donkey walk with the donkey kick. Repeat the bear walk, but now, the child transfers weight to their hands to occasionally kick up with the legs: first the right leg and then the left. The object is to kick up approximately 90 degrees. With the kicks, encourage the child to bray like a donkey: *Hee-haw!* (Be sure there's enough space so nothing accidentally gets kicked.)

Amy: Self-Regulation

Amy is a highly intelligent eleven-year-old girl who attends fifth grade at a public charter school and is enrolled in a gifted and talented program. She has a lot of difficulty with self-regulation. She behaves well in school, often because she enjoys learning so much. She has trouble when she gets home. Her parents notice that once she steps off the bus, she begins to spin and twirl. She really likes swinging high on her jungle gym swing. She also likes to jump high and fast on the family trampoline. When it's time to come in and do homework, she has difficulty calming down. She is typically so riled up by the exercise that she can't come back into the house for at least another half hour.

Amy's mother was curious about why her daughter could be so functional at school but was unable to focus at home. The family consulted an occupational therapist, who diagnosed Amy with sensory processing disorder: sensory seeking. Amy can inhibit these needs at school because she's hyperfocused on learning. At home, she needs a lot of sensory input.

The therapist helped the family create a transition plan. The therapist recommended giving Amy a five-minute heads-up notice when it's time to go inside. She is allowed to play for four more minutes any way she wants. When there is one minute left before going inside, Amy's mother yells out one of her favorite animals. Amy then walks around like that animal. She especially likes animal walks that involve going on all fours. She can do the bear walk or crab walk for 100 feet. There's also a mat outside where Amy can practice animal walks that require her to slither and creep. Once she enters the house, she drinks a glass of water. All this time outside helps her focus on her homework without fussing or needing more movement.

Hop and Jump Animal Walks

These animal walks allow for hopping and jumping, which kids enjoy immensely. Jumping also improves balance and coordination. A favorite part of this activity is to imitate the animal noise, so don't forget to add the sound that the animal makes.

ACTIVITY TYPE: Deep pressure, Heavy work, Total body strength

Directions:

1. Do the kangaroo hop. Have the child stand upright with both feet together. (Be sure feet remain together at all times.) Instruct them to bend their elbows so that their hands come up to their shoulders, like a kangaroo's short arms. The child then hops forward, keeping both feet together, and lets their hands flop up and down. Remind the child that kangaroos hop far, sometimes 2 to 3 feet per hop. Challenge them to see how high and far they can hop. To make this more difficult and add some heavy work, have the child wear a pouch around their waist (a "pouch for joey") and stuff it with a wrist weight.

2. Do the elephant stomp. Have the child stand upright and clasp their hands together by interlocking fingers to make an elephant trunk, allowing the arms to hang. Now the child stomps their feet, one in front of the other, heavily and with large steps. Let the "trunk" sway back and forth. Encourage the child to trumpet like an elephant. To make this more difficult, have the child cross their arms in front of them and stomp around in circles while still moving forward.

3. Do the penguin waddle. Have the child stand upright with their feet facing outward, shoulder-distance apart. Have them imagine that they are walking on thin ice. Let them know that if they spread their feet out, they are less likely to fall through. Have the child extend their hands outward like a penguin's flippers, bend their knees, and shuffle from side to side to waddle forward. Encourage them to take short steps from side to side. To make this more difficult, you can use a TheraBand around the child's knees.

TIP: In a safe, uncluttered space, the child can do any of the animal walks backward.

Belly-Down Animal Walks

This activity allows children to imagine that they are animals moving around on their bellies. Slithering and sliding on the tummy promotes proprioception, calming, tactile input, and relaxation. Lying down lets their whole body feel the movement rather than just their arms and legs. A favorite part of this activity is to imitate the animal noise, so don't forget to add the sound that the animal makes.

ACTIVITY TYPE: Cardiovascular workout, Deep pressure, Heavy work, Proprioception, Total body strength

What You'll Need:

- Gym mats (optional)

- Comfortable, loose clothing that can get dirty

- Gloves (optional)

Directions:

1. Have the child lie on their tummy.

2. Do the seal walk. Have the child lift their upper body by pushing off the floor with their hands. Their head should be upright with their legs and feet flat on the ground. They can flop forward by moving their hands one at a time, the way a seal would. Remind them not to use their legs for propulsion, only the power of their arms. Encourage them to make the sound a seal makes: *Arf! Arf!* To make this more difficult, have the child push a playground ball forward with their nose or body while moving forward.

3. Do the snake slither. Using their right arm and leg, the child pulls themselves forward and slithers like a snake. Encourage them to make the

sound a snake makes: *Sssssss.* Repeat with the left arm and leg. Snakes also move in a side-winding pattern. This activity provides a lot of heavy work and tactile input from the floor, and children will most likely tire out easily from pulling their bodies on the ground.

4. Do the lizard walk. Using the opposite side arm and leg, the child pulls themselves forward while keeping their tummy on the floor. Creeping forward like a lizard has a lot of total-body heavy work. As the child gets stronger, they can crawl longer distances.

TIP: All animal walks can be made progressively more challenging. Start by having the child follow a path 15 feet long. As the child gets stronger and builds endurance, they can move farther, up to 30 or 40 feet. It's also fun to create an obstacle course by having the child walk over pillows and crash pads for more of a challenge.

Find the Hidden Treasure

This play dough activity (with "hidden treasures" folded inside) provides endless opportunity for fine-motor strengthening through exercising the small muscles in the hands. While you can purchase Play-Doh, this is an easy and inexpensive recipe to make at home. Both recipes provided are safe for children to make with you, which gives the child additional input.

ACTIVITY TYPE: Fine motor, Hand strength, Heavy work, Messy play, Tactile

SAFETY TIP: When using edible play dough, portion out the dough for each child to use individually. Previously used dough should be discarded. Also make sure the child's hands are thoroughly washed before and after the play dough activity. This is especially important if using the edible play dough recipe or if multiple children will be using the same play dough.

What You'll Need:

- Play-Doh or homemade dough (see DIY Tips on page 101)

- Small objects like coated paper clips, small plastic toys, beads larger than ½ inch, character erasers, etc., to use as treasure

Directions:

1. Make a ball with the dough and then flatten it out into a disk. You can use a rolling pin or just smoosh it with your palms. Place a few small treasure objects on the dough disc and fold the dough over to cover them. Reshape into a ball.

2. Supervise the child as they hunt through the dough for treasure.

3. To give the individual fingers more of a challenge, instruct the child to use only 2 fingers to find the hidden treasure. Start by using the thumb and index finger. Next use thumb and middle finger, followed by the thumb and ring fingers, and finally the thumb and small finger.

4. When finished, remove any additional small objects from the dough.

5. Store the dough in an airtight container to play with another day.

TIP: Dough kept in the refrigerator will remain moist longer. If it dries out, add a small amount of water and knead it back to the correct consistency. Discard any leftover edible play dough and discard any dough with white spots (mold).

DIY TIP FOR HOMEMADE DOUGH: Combine 2 cups all-purpose flour, ¾ cup salt, 4 teaspoons cream of tartar, 2 cups lukewarm water, 2 tablespoons vegetable oil, and a few drops of food coloring in a quart-size airtight plastic bag or plastic container. Ask your child to mix all the ingredients together until dough forms. The child can use their hands for extra messy play, or they can use a spoon. If the dough is too sticky, add more flour.

DIY TIP FOR HOMEMADE EDIBLE DOUGH: Combine 1 cup creamy peanut butter, 1 cup powdered sugar, ½ cup powdered milk, and ¼ to ⅓ cup honey. Mix the ingredients in a quart-size airtight plastic bag or plastic container. If the dough is too sticky, add more powdered sugar.

Sensory Box

A sensory box includes items to offer a child a sensory break no matter where they are. Sensory boxes make up an important part of the sensory diet (see page 17) and contents can be changed based on interest, sensory input needed, and environment. I also like including a belt bag (waist pouch) in the sensory box, as it can be worn by your child or kept in their room or desk at school and used as needed. This is a good activity for parents to share with their child's teacher and school support team. At home, a sensory box is helpful for rainy days and times when it's difficult to go outdoors and play.

ACTIVITY TYPE: Proprioceptive, Tactile

SAFETY TIP: If the child tends to put small objects in their mouth, do not use anything that could be a choking hazard.

What You'll Need:
- Large plastic bin

- Belt bag (waist pouch)

- Various fidget toys, such as rubber bands, squishy balls, stress balls, plastic snake toys, plastic coins, and play dough (see page 101 for DIY instructions)

- Mouth toys, such as chewy tubes, chewy necklaces, etc.

Directions:
1. Fill the bin and belt bag with fidget and mouth toys that provide sensory input. If the belt bag is to be used in the classroom, make sure to provide toys that are not distracting to other children.

2. Review the items in the box and belt bag with the child.

3. Have them hold and look at each item and ask how and when they might use it. The idea is to help the child self-identify when to take a break and what type of break is needed for the particular situation.

TIP: At school, a sensory box can be stored in the back of the classroom or cubby and taken out during a sensory break. The belt bag (waist pouch) is smaller and more portable. The child can bring their belt bag in a car, while shopping, or during other activities where they need to stay in just the right zone.

Creamy Creations

This is a good art activity and provides tactile input. The wonderful texture and smell of thick shaving cream gives sensory input and helps the sensory seeker experience more input so that they can focus. The child can spread out the shaving cream on a cookie tray or flat surface and play with it. It's also possible to build igloos, snowmen, or a whole variety of shapes. Even though this is messy, it is also a calming activity and fun for children of all ages. It's also a great way to practice copying shapes, numbers, and letters. I often use this activity to enhance my lessons on correct letter formation.

ACTIVITY TYPE: Messy play, Tactile

SAFETY TIP: Supervise the child closely so they do not put the shaving cream in their mouth.

What You'll Need:

- Painting smock

- Shaving cream in a can (the smellier and thicker the better)

- Cookie tray or other flat surface

- Paper towels

- Access to a bathroom for washing up

Directions:

1. Have the child wash their hands thoroughly and put on their smock.

2. Invite the child to remove the cap from the shaving cream can and spray a lot onto their cookie sheet or other surface.

3. Show the child how to put their hands into the cream and spread it out evenly. At first it will feel cold and squishy. Discuss the feelings, like cold, soft, smooth, and silky. Sniff the cream and identify the scent.

4. Encourage the child to put their hands into the cream, spreading it out evenly over the whole surface.

CONTINUED

5. Invite the child to use their pointer finger to draw simple shapes (circle, square, triangle), letters, and numbers in the cream. (Older children can practice writing words.) You can also help the child build shapes, such as a snowman or a house. Be creative; suggest building something the child is interested in.

6. When the child is done playing, wipe the shaving cream off their hands with paper towels. Put the towels in the trash and avoiding touching other surfaces on the way to wash up.

7. Wash thoroughly.

TIP: I like going to a dollar store for inexpensive shaving cream, as the more expensive brands don't translate to a better experience.

VARIATION: Use cornstarch and water instead of shaving cream. The concept is the same, but the texture is silkier. For this variation, use a cookie sheet with at least 1-inch sides. Mix together 1 cup of cornstarch with 1 tablespoon of water in the cookie sheet. Add more water to make it easier to mix and move around, if desired. You can also add a few drops of food coloring for variety.

Treasure Hunt

Playing in a bin with rice is a wonderful way to promote tactile awareness and stereognosis (the ability to identify an object without using your eyes).

ACTIVITY TYPE: Messy play, Stereognosis, Tactile

SAFETY TIPS: Do not use any toys that are sharp or sticky. This activity is not recommended for children who put objects in their mouths. Be aware that some of these toys may be choking hazards and the child needs to be supervised at all times.

What You Need:

- Plastic bin, approximately 1 foot by 2 feet by 6 inches

- Rice to fill the bin

- Small plastic objects such as buttons, plastic toys, coated paper clips, clothespins, coins, plastic utensils, etc.

Directions:

1. Have the child wash their hands thoroughly with soap and water, and dry hands completely.

2. Invite the child to sit at a table and chair that supports the child to have their feet on the ground, knees at 90 degrees, and arms on the table with elbows bent to 90 degrees. This position helps with proprioception (knowing where your body is in space), and keeps their feet grounded on the floor.

3. Introduce the activity. Review the rules to always keep the rice in the bin and to never put the rice in their mouth.

4. Open up the rice bin and invite the child to smell the rice. Discuss the smells.

CONTINUED

5. Show the child how to put their hands in and move the rice around, scooping, smoothing, and digging in deep.

6. Next show the child the small toys, one at a time. Identify each item and discuss the texture, shape, and weight. For example, a paper clip is hard, long, has rounded ends, is lightweight, and is about one inch long.

7. After discussing each item, have the child close their eyes while you hide the objects in the rice bin.

8. Next, invite the child to put their hands in the rice and find the items. No peeking! Once they find an object, ask the child to describe it and identify what it is.

9. When all items are found, reverse roles. Invite the child to hide the objects for you to find and identify.

VARIATION: **Instead of rice, use dried beans (great northern beans, pinto beans, kidney beans, etc.). Each type of bean provides a different tactile feeling. The directions remain the same.**

Cat and Cow Stretch

The Cat-Cow yoga stretch (Chakravakasana) helps lengthen and relax the back. A cow stretches its back down toward the ground, while a cat stretches its back upward. The child gets to practice doing both and has fun alternating between mooing and meowing.

ACTIVITY TYPE: Mindfulness

What You'll Need:

- Yoga mat

- Comfortable, stretchy clothing

Directions:

1. Instruct the child to kneel on the mat and sit on their feet with their toes pointing behind them. Have them separate their knees a little and lean forward, placing their hands in front of them. (This position is called quadruped.)

2. Encourage the child to breathe in slowly without rushing. Tell them to imagine that there's a string attached to their back that's being pulled from above. Their shoulders, arms, and legs remain still while their back bends upward like a cat. Instruct the child to breathe out slowly for 5 counts. Encourage them to meow like a cat.

3. Now, the "string" is released and is being pulled from below. Instruct the child to move their tummy toward the ground, while breathing in slowly. Have the child hold the stretch for 5 counts and encourage them to moo like a cow.

4. Have the child repeat the cat and cow stretches 5 times. Ask them to notice how their back feels with each stretch. Briefly mention that cats like to explore and crawl around. Ask, "If you were a cat, what type of cat would you be?" Then briefly mention that cows stand still while grazing on grass. Ask, "Can you stay still for a few minutes? What does being still feel like?"

TIP: A blanket under the knees can provide extra cushioning, if needed.

Light Rest

The end of a yoga practice is spent resting in a position called Savasana. It's said to be the most important part of yoga. It may be difficult to get a squirmy, silly, or fidgety child to relax and lie still. One idea is to suggest they pretend to be a dead bug lying on its back with its limbs in the air and then have the child flop their arms and legs to the ground.

ACTIVITY TYPE: Mindfulness

What You'll Need:

- Dimly lit room with no distracting noises

- Yoga mat

- Eye pillow or soft cloth

- Weighted blanket (optional)

- Guided visualization (see A Trip to the Ocean on page 113 or Progressive Relaxation on page 116 for suggested scripts)

Directions:

1. Let the child choose their position on the mat. They can lie on their back, on their side, or even on their tummy. If using, cover them with the weighted blanket.

2. Invite the child to close their eyes or use the eye pillow or soft cloth. Let the child know that for the next few minutes they will be letting their body relax.

3. Help relax their mind by reading the guided visualization.

Push!

Pushing against a Lycra compression loop offers a lot of resistance in the direction of the push. It's fun because children start out very small, in a crouched position, and then PUSH very hard to stand up and spread out their arms and legs. Proprioception helps with strength, especially as they extend/push outward. The softness of the Lycra is calming and feels good on their hands.

ACTIVITY TYPE: Heavy work, Proprioception

What You'll Need:
- Commercial Lycra compression loop or DIY (see page 72)

Directions:
1. Invite the child to place their feet inside the compression loop and stand on it. Instruct them to crouch and raise their hands just above their head, and drape the top of the loop over them, so they're crouched in the center of it.

2. When the child is ready, shout, "PUSH!" The child should try to stand up in the loop and push their arms out, and then return to the crouching position.

3. Whisper, "Push." Again, the child stands and pushes. Notice if there's a difference in their effort and fun.

4. Keep varying how you say, "Push," and continue the game for at least 5 to 10 minutes.

VARIATIONS: To engage different muscles, vary the position of pushing by having the child lie on their back and push outward. Next try having them lie on their tummy in a curled-up ball and push out to a flat position. Next have them kneel in the loop and push up.

Calm Breathing

In yoga, pranayama is the practice of breathing. Breathing is very important for calming oneself. In fact, in yoga, breathing is more important than the poses (asanas). Breathing in a focused manner helps with instant calming and balances your energy.

ACTIVITY TYPE: Mindfulness

What You'll Need:
- Quiet room free of distractions (no TV or distracting noises in the background)

Directions:
1. Familiarize yourself with the movements and practice doing them before leading the child in this exercise.

2. Say the following script to your child:

   Find a comfortable place to sit.

   Raise your right hand and place your thumb on one side of your nose, your index and middle fingers on your forehead, and your ring finger lightly on your left nostril.

   Close off the right nostril with your thumb. Breathe in through the left nostril for 4 counts.

   Close your left nostril with the right ring finger. Hold this briefly.

   Open your right nostril and breathe out for 6 counts.

   Breathe in deeply through the right nostril for 4 counts.

   Close right nostril with thumb. Keep both nostrils closed briefly.

   Open the left nostril and breathe out for 6 counts.

TIP: The child should lightly hold their nose closed but with enough pressure to prevent air from slipping out.

Jack: Anxiety

Jack is a five-year-old boy who attends kindergarten at a public school. He is a smart and very sweet natured. He also tends to get very anxious, especially about time and schedules. His mother reports that he does not notice pain; when he gets anxious, he hides in his bedroom or bathroom and will suck on his arm until he is bruised or bleeding. Jack is also working with a psychologist who is teaching him meditation to help him feel calm and relaxed.

The psychologist began working with Jack weekly. At first, Jack had difficulty with deep breathing techniques. He didn't like the feeling of air going up and down in his nose. The instructor taught him alternate-nostril breathing. Initially this was hard to coordinate. With practice, he figured out how to switch his thumb and ring finger, to inhale on one side of his nostril and exhale on the other. He could repeat the pattern four times and found that he felt calmer and more focused. He even reported feeling happy following this new breath pattern, and he began cracking jokes.

Since learning the breathing exercises was helpful in decreasing Jack's anxiety, his parents and occupational therapist decided to integrate it into regularly scheduled sensory breaks. They met with his schoolteacher and explained that Jack would need a quick sensory break every thirty minutes, or sooner if he was acting anxious. The teacher liked this idea immensely. She allowed Jack to go to the back of the room every half hour with the classroom aide. There he used his sensory box to find an activity that changed his engine speed. The teacher also began to integrate deep breathing into her morning routine. She discovered that all of her students felt better and were more ready to sit and learn afterward.

Chair Push-ups

Isometric exercises are contractions of muscles where the body doesn't noticeably move or change position. Chair push-ups help strengthen the body without the need to move around. This is an especially good activity in spaces that don't allow for a lot of movement, such as in a classroom where the child is wiggly and therefore unable to concentrate.

ACTIVITY TYPE: Heavy work, Proprioception, Upper-body strength

What You'll Need:

- A sturdy chair

Directions:

1. Have the child sit upright on a chair and place their hands on the seat right next to their hips, with their palms down on the chair and elbows bent up to 90 degrees. Their feet can remain on the floor.

2. Ask them to take in a deep breath and lift their bottom off the chair by extending their arms.

3. Start by completing 5 repetitions twice a day. As the child gets stronger, increase this to 10 repetitions 3 times a day.

TIP: For an extra challenge, instruct the child to lift their feet off the floor as well.

A Trip to the Ocean

This activity takes the child on a faraway trip through meditation and mindfulness without having to leave your space. The first part of the practice, the warm-up period, helps the child relax and use their imagination to join in the activity more fully. The second part involves a fun hands-on activity. The third is the actual gentle relaxation period. The follow-up activity asks the child to reflect on the experience.

ACTIVITY TYPE: Mindfulness

What You'll Need:

- Quiet room free of distractions (no TV or distracting noises in the background)

- Pictures of the ocean or a library book about the ocean

- Various ocean-related items (sand, sand toys, shells, blanket, sunglasses, etc.)

- Towel or mat

- Drawing paper

- Crayons or markers

Directions:

1. Prepare yourself for this activity by consciously relaxing. Throughout this activity, speak in a low tone with regular pauses.

2. Show the child the photos of the ocean or read from the book about the ocean, sharing the pictures in the book.

3. Discuss how a trip to the ocean might proceed: How would you get there? In a car? By airplane? By foot?

4. Examine the items you might use or see if you were at the ocean. Discuss the items, focusing on their characteristics (size, smell, shape, color, etc.).

5. Now invite the child to lie on a towel or mat.

CONTINUED

6. Using a calm voice and slow-paced speech, invite the child to join you at the beach. Read the following script:

Welcome, [child's name] I'm so glad you joined me today. I want you to imagine that you are at the beach. In your mind's eye, visualize walking toward the sand. The sun is shining. Look up and you will see the sky is clear, shiny blue. There's a bird overhead, just flying lazily toward the water. Notice how he flies, slowly, with his wings going up and down with the gentle breeze.

As you step forward, you feel sand on your feet. The sand is warm and feels very comfortable. Notice how it feels in between your toes. Now, lean over and pick up sand in your hands. Notice there are a lot of sand particles, each one a tiny piece that rests in your palm.

As you walk farther, notice the sound of the ocean waves, gently moving forward and backward, forward and backward on the shore. You feel peaceful, and you start to match your breath to the waves.

Breathe in, and hold it. [Pause for 3 to 5 seconds while the child holds their breath.] Breathe out. Breathe in the warm, positive energy; breathe out the negative energy. [Pause.] Breathe in, hold it, [pause] breathe out. Breathe in, hold it, [pause] breathe out.

As you inhale, imagine your favorite color. It might be blue or red or yellow or some other color.

As you exhale, say to yourself a favorite word. It might be "love," or "happiness," or "peace." Breathe in, hold it. [Pause.] Breathe out. Breathe in and [pause] breathe out. Breathe in, hold it. [Pause] Breathe out. Breathe in, hold it. [Pause.] Breathe out.

Take a moment to notice how you feel. [Pause.]

We are now going to walk back up the beach, slowly getting ready to return here. Take a deep breath and begin to wiggle your fingers and toes. When you are ready, sit up slowly.

Know that you can always come back to this place. [Pause] If your eyes are closed, open them whenever you are ready. Notice how you feel fully alert yet very relaxed.

7. After the guided meditation, invite the child to draw a picture about this trip to the ocean. Afterward, discuss the drawing to help orient the child back to the here and now. Allow them time to describe their imaginary journey.

TIP: Overhead lighting can be very distracting, especially if it's from fluorescent bulbs. It's best to turn off lighting altogether and just allow natural sunlight in. If that's not possible or practical, then use a lower light (LED) bulb. Another option is to give the child an eye pillow or eye mask to wear. This helps decrease any distractions from the environment and lets them focus on the actual meditation.

VARIATION: The trip to the ocean can be varied based on your child's interests. Maybe they would like to take a walk in the forest or hike up a mountain. The photos, book, and items you choose would correspond to that place.

Progressive Relaxation

Children under stress often don't remember what it's like to feel relaxed. Progressive relaxation allows children to notice the difference between relaxed and tensed muscles. Eventually, the child will learn how to relax their muscles without this structured mindfulness activity.

ACTIVITY TYPE: Mindfulness

What You'll Need:

- Quiet room free of distractions (no TV or distracting noises in the background)

- Towel or mat

- Eye pillow or soft cloth to cover eyes (optional)

Directions:

1. Prepare yourself for this activity by consciously relaxing. Throughout this activity, speak in a low tone with regular pauses to set a relaxing mood.

2. Welcome the child and make sure they feel safe and secure in this place. Give them permission to relax and assure them that you are here to keep them safe. Let them know you will make sure they will be done on time and that there's nowhere else they need to go and nothing else to think about.

3. Invite the child to remove their shoes and lie down on a towel or mat.

4. While they are lying down, invite the child to close their eyes. They may want to use an eye pillow or soft cloth to cover their eyes.

5. Lead the child through a gentle preparation for relaxation. Start by inviting them to breathe, just breathe. Slow down the breathing by teaching them to breathe in for four counts and out for six counts. Take this step very slowly and calmly, demonstrating how to breathe and count in your head, rather than out loud. Repeat this four to five times until the child appears to be slowing down.

6.   Start at the bottom of the body and work your way up. In order, ask the child to do the following:

     a.   Clench their toes, hold for 5 seconds, and release. Repeat 3 to 4 times.

     b.   Clench calves and legs, hold for 5 seconds, and release. Repeat 3 to 4 times.

     c.   Breathe in for 5 seconds and out for 7 seconds. Repeat 4 to 5 times.

     d.   Clench the butt and tummy muscles, hold for 5 seconds, and release. Repeat 3 to 4 times.

     e.   Clench the shoulder and chest muscles, hold for 5 seconds, and release. Repeat 3 to 4 times.

     f.   Make a tight fist, hold for 5 seconds, and release.

     g.   Scrunch up their face tightly, close their eyes, and purse their lips, hold for 5 seconds, and release. Repeat 3 to 4 times.

     h.   Curl into a tight ball using all the muscles in their body, hold for 5 seconds, and release. Repeat this 3 to 4.

7.   Now, invite the child to just lie there and relax, enjoying this feeling of complete relaxation. Ask them to notice what it feels like to be at rest and how different this is from tightening their muscles.

8.   Tell the child you are now going to slowly return to this room. Instruct the child to take a deep breath and begin to wiggle their fingers and toes.

9.   When they are ready, have the child sit up slowly and open their eyes. Have them notice that they are feeling fully alert yet very relaxed.

Rock Pose

Rock pose is just another name for Child's Pose (Balasana), which is a wonderful relaxation pose that can be done almost anywhere there's space on the ground.

ACTIVITY TYPE: Mindfulness

What You'll Need:

- Yoga mat

- Comfortable, stretchy clothing

Directions:

1. Invite the child to kneel on the mat and then sit back on their feet with toes pointing behind them.

2. Instruct the child to take a deep breath in, separate their knees a little, and lean forward.

3. Have them lay their arms alongside their hips and rest their head on the mat.

4. Encourage the child to breathe slowly without rushing. Instruct them to breathe in for 4 counts and breathe out for 6 counts. Allow them to stay in this position for a few minutes, breathing in and out.

5. To add some interest, have the child imagine that they are a rock. You can say, "Imagine that you are a rock. What type of rock would you be? Rocks have to stay still for a very long time. Can you stay still for a few minutes? What does being still feel like?"

TIP: To get into a "rock" mind-set, walk around a playground or backyard with your child. Help them search for a rock that's about 3 or 4 inches in size. Once the child finds a rock, have them examine it for details. Discuss the shape of the rock, as well as the texture, temperature, and color. Is it one color or layers of colors? Does it have sharp edges or smooth surfaces? Does it smell? After examining the rock, have the child put it back where they found it.

VARIATION: To do an Extended Rock pose, have the child separate their knees enough to allow their body to rest on the mat and extend their hands out in front of them.

Jordan: Body Awareness

Jordan is an eight-year-old girl who is home-schooled. She has a habit of crashing, banging, and bumping into people and things. This makes learning in a school very difficult. She also has difficulty taking turns in conversations with others. She prefers to talk about her favorite topic, dinosaurs. She knows everything about these prehistoric animals, and she likes to weave a fun fact into most conversations.

Jordan attended occupational therapy to help understand where her body is in space and to minimize her need to crash and bump all the time. Jordan's therapist introduced her to a yoga teacher who works with children with sensory processing disorder. Her parents created a yoga activity board. Jordan especially liked being able to create a sequence of moves and follow the pattern. However, she was fidgeting all the time, and the yoga teacher couldn't get Jordan to breathe and stay focused on the lesson.

The occupational therapist decided to take a different approach to yoga. She asked Jordan more about her favorite dinosaurs, and she had a lot to share. She described all her favorite prehistoric animal friends with excitement. The yoga teacher took this information very seriously. At the next session, the yoga teacher had a variety of dinosaur-related picture cards to put on the yoga activity board. She also brought plastic dinosaur figures and asked Jordan to hold on to them during certain moves. This way she had to focus on the move and holding on to the toy.

At the end of the session, they practiced the Rock Pose, which the yoga teacher called the "dinosaur resting" pose for fun. She had Jordan lie on her mat with her favorite dinosaur, the triceratops. Jordan put on her "dinosaur feet" (slippers) so she would remain still. For the first time, Jordan learned how to be still and breathe in "like a dinosaur."

Good Morning, Sun

This series of moves is called "sun salutation" and has been adapted for children. I call it the "Good Morning, Sun" routine. This sequence of steps lets the child use each joint of their body for stretching, strengthening, and weight-bearing. While this is a common sequence, the routine can be varied and other stretches included.

ACTIVITY TYPE: Heavy work, Mindfulness

What You'll Need:

- Yoga mat

- Stretchy, comfortable clothing

Directions:

1. Practice this sequence on your own until you have it down so that you can demonstrate it to your child and/or do it along with them.

   Instruct the child as follows:

2. Stand straight with your feet together, shoulders back, hands down by your sides, and look forward. Breathe in deeply and raise your arms overhead. Say, "Good morning, Sun!"

3. Exhale deeply, and swan dive down to a forward fold by floating your arms down to your sides and bending over. Look up so that you can see in front of you and make your back flat enough to balance an imaginary teacup on your back.

4. Return to the forward fold and put your hands on the ground. Bring your right leg behind you, and lift up your arms to both side of your head.

5. Breathe in. Return your hands to the ground and bring your other leg back to make a plank. Breathe out. Push down so your entire body is on the ground. Breathe in. Push on the ground with your arms to straighten them out and raise your head (Upward Dog).

CONTINUED

6. Breathe out. Raise up your bottom so that your body makes an upside-down V (Downward Dog).

7. Breathe in. Bring your right foot forward into a lunge. Then bring your left foot forward so that you are in a forward fold again.

8. Reverse swan dive up by tightening your tummy, lifting your body up with a straight back, and float your arms back up to the top of your body.

9. (Repeat steps 2 to 7, stepping back now with the left leg in step 4.)

TIP: You can view this sequence as well as other yoga poses and sequences by searching on YouTube to help clarify the directions, if necessary.

Upside-Down Bicycle Ride

The bicycle (or shoulder stand) is a powerful yoga pose that's easy for children to perform. Inversion poses help stimulate the thyroid gland and relieve stress and depression. They also improve digestion. The shoulder stand strengthens all the body's muscles, including the legs, bottom, abdominal muscles, and arms.

ACTIVITY TYPE: Heavy work, Mindfulness, Vestibular

What You'll Need:

- Yoga mat

- Comfortable, stretchy clothing

Directions:

1. Instruct the child to sit upright with legs curled into their body and their arms holding themselves in a tight ball.

2. Using their momentum and core strength, instruct the child to rock themselves back and forth like a ball 3 to 4 times, stopping with their feet overhead and their arms supporting their body.

3. Guide the child in lifting up their leg so they are vertical while their upper body remains horizontal on the ground. Be sure the child keeps their neck straight with their eyes looking at the ceiling.

4. Instruct the child to breathe calmly while their feet are elevated and to hold this position for 3 to 4 seconds.

5. Now, invite the child to take an upside-down bicycle ride by pedaling their feet in a circle. Have them do this for 10 rotations forward and then backward.

6. When the child is ready to "get off the bike," have them return to a sitting position by lowering their legs and using their momentum to sit up all the way.

TIP: Challenge the child to stay upside down with their legs lifted for a longer period.

The Pretzel

Yoga poses that get the child to twist help with posture and stress reduction. These poses help open up the chest, shoulders, and back. They also help release stored-up tension. Children love turning themselves into a pretzel.

ACTIVITY TYPE: Mindfulness

What You'll Need:

- Yoga mat

- Comfortable, stretchy clothing

Directions:

1. Turn the lights down to a comfortable level, and invite the child to sit on the mat with their legs straight out.

2. Instruct the child to bend their right knee so that it's pointing toward the sky and bring their right heel as close to their bottom as comfortable.

3. Now, have them lift their right leg in its bent position to the other side of their left leg. The child can bend their left leg as if sitting cross-legged or leave it straight out. (The child can try to bend their left leg so that the knee is pointing toward the sky and try to line up their knees.)

4. Ask the child to sit up as straight as possible in this position, as if a string on their head is being pulled toward the ceiling.

5. Ask the child to look over their right shoulder and place their right hand behind their back and their left hand on their right knee.

6. Prompt the child to breathe in, and see if they can look a bit farther behind their back.

7. While the child is holding the pose, ask, "Do you feel like a pretzel?" The child can now unwind their pretzel slowly.

8. Repeat the steps on the opposite side.

Yoga Activity Board & Practice

This activity involves making a poster that illustrates a variety of yoga sequences. I use a poster like this to help children visualize a six-step yoga flow pattern. The pictures should be colorful and easy to see as well as interchangeable. You can add or take away poses, and challenge the child to complete the sequence without your assistance. Children really like the variety and the self-determination of this activity.

ACTIVITY TYPE: Mindfulness, Motor planning, Visual tracking

What You'll Need:

- Foam board, 1.5 by 2.5 feet

- Pen

- Glue

- Colored strips of paper printed with the words "Yoga Time" and "Can You Follow the Pattern"

- 24 to 30 ½-inch sticky Velcro circles

- Two identical pictures or illustrations of 12 to 15 basic yoga moves

- 12 or 15 3-by-5 index cards

- Yoga mat

Directions:

1. Start by making the yoga activity board. Draw 4 straight, horizontal lines across the foam board in its vertical position spaced evenly apart.

2. Glue the "Yoga Time" paper strip centered from left to right at the top of the board.

3. Stick 6 Velcro circles in the top row spaced evenly apart.

4. Below this, glue the "Can you follow the pattern?" paper strip.

5. Add three additional lines of 6 Velcro strips spaced evenly apart to cover the board.

CONTINUED

6. To prepare the yoga cards, paste the yoga illustrations onto the index cards. Print the name of the yoga pose on the back of each card and laminate if possible to make them last longer. Stick a Velcro circle fastener on the back of each card.

7. To play the game, choose a sequence of 6 cards. Start with 1 or 2 sitting or standing poses, 1 breathing exercise, 2 stronger standing poses, and 1 or 2 lying-down poses. The last pose should be a still, quiet pose for the final rest.

8. Stick the cards in the sequence on the first row of Velcro circles.

9. Lead the child on their mat through the 6-pose sequence. Have them practice each pose.

10. Allow the child to sort through the cards and ask them to attach an identical row on the second set of Velcro dots. Ask the child to follow the pattern without your help. Using only finger pointing, have child move through all 6 poses. Try to limit verbal or physical prompts.

11. Once one series of 6 poses is mastered, add additional poses in the remaining rows until all the Velcro circles have been covered and the child can follow all the poses on the activity board without direction.

My colleague Yvette Hernandez, OTR/L, created this activity.

Rope Tunnel

For this activity, the child is suspended in the air, requiring them to balance while they are moving forward and backward. Vestibular input is primarily provided by forward and backward motion, with some input from side-to-side motion. This tunnel is suspended between trees outdoors and rocks back and forth with every movement.

ACTIVITY TYPE: Heavy work, Vestibular

SAFETY TIPS: Be sure to check the weight limit on the tunnel and make sure the child falls within the acceptable range. Attach the tunnel safely between two trees or poles without rocks or people underneath.

What You'll Need:

- Netted rope tunnel, such as the Rope Tunnel Bridge by HearthSong (or see Alternative Equipment below)

Directions:

1. Have the child climb into the rope tunnel and crawl through. This takes a lot of upper-body strength and endurance, as the bottom is off the ground.

2. Have the child crawl forward and then go back using a backward crawl.

ALTERNATIVE EQUIPMENT: Don't have a rope net tunnel? It's possible to do this activity on a balance beam, which is closer to the ground. The child can crawl onto the balance beam and move forward or backward, or stand up and walk sideways. For safety purposes, I prefer balance beams that are within 6 to 12 inches from the ground. Another alternative is to use a solid-walled play tunnel and have the child crawl through while two adults hold on to the ends and move the tunnel around in asymmetrical and arrhythmic motions to challenge the balance of the child.

Resources for Parents

Therapist Directory

STAR Institute for Sensory Processing Disorder Treatment Directory
www.spdstar.org/treatment-directory. This online resource can help you find
therapists across the US who have specific training in SPD.

Curriculums to Teach Self-Regulation

The Alert Program: Self-Regulation Made Easy! by Mary Sue Williams and Shelly
Shellenberger
This is a powerful curriculum that teaches self-regulation. Their books include
Test Drive: Introducing the Alert Program Through Song and *Take Five! Staying
Alert at Home and School.*

Superflex: A Superhero Social Thinking Curriculum Package by Stephanie Madrigal and Michelle Garcia Winner
This two-book set helps teach self-regulation in relationships. This is a fun
program that helps children become their own superheroes and use new skills to
overcome a team of "unthinkable" behaviors.

The Zones of Regulation by Leah Kuypers
This program helps by identifying emotions as green, red, blue, or yellow zones
and offers many strategies to cope with feelings in these zones.

Therapist-Directed Interventions for Specific SPD Conditions

The following are resources for therapist-directed interventions for specific SPD
conditions. Check out the websites for specific techniques to find professionals
who have expertise in these specialty areas. The websites listed here are operated
by nationally based businesses who support children with SPD.

Auditory

Therapeutic Listening is an evidence-based modulated music therapy program. Children wear headphones, listening to modulated music while doing gross-motor activities. This decreases auditory defensiveness and auditory-filtering difficulties. You can learn more about the program at www:vitallinks.com.

Interoception

To watch an excellent video on interoception, as explained by occupational therapists from the STAR Center, visit: www.facebook.com/STARInstituteforSPD/videos/1540367686031185/.

Oral

Beckman Oral Motor Protocol is an intensive oral motor therapy technique aimed to desensitize the mouth and face. When implemented by a trained occupational therapist or speech and language pathologist, it may assist with oral apraxia, oral tactile defensiveness, and picky-eating tendencies. You can find more information at www.beckmanoralmotor.com.

Tactile

Wilbarger Deep Pressure Proprioceptive Technique (DPPT) is a brushing program created by Patricia Wilbarger to decrease sensory defensiveness. The parents can implement this intervention at home under the direction of a trained occupational therapist. Parents use a special brush on the skin, followed by joint compressions. This process takes up to five minutes per session and results in desensitization of the child's skin. This is a highly effective intervention and relatively easy to implement. If interested, speak with an occupational therapist.

Visual

For more information on Irlen syndrome, visit www.irlensyndrome.org. This condition results from the brain's inability to process/filter visual information. This problem tends to be hereditary and cannot be identified by standardized assessments (educational, psychological, optometric, or medical testing). Symptoms include reading problems, headaches, light sensitivity, attentional and concentration problems, eye fatigue and strain, difficulty with depth perception, and distortions in print or environment.

Further Information

Still have questions? I'm happy to answer them. Visit www.kidswork.biz for more resources and research on sensory processing disorder and occupational therapy.

References

American Psychiatric Association. *Diagnostic and Statistical Manual of Mental Disorders*. Washington, D.C: American Psychiatric Association, 2013.

Ayres, A. Jean. *Sensory Integration and Learning Disorders*. Los Angeles, CA: Western Psychological Services, 1973.

Blanche, E. I., S. C. Bodison, Leah Stein Duker, and Sharon Cermak. "An examination of sensory-related terminology across disciplines: part two." *SIS Quarterly Practice Connections* 23, no. 1 (August 2019): 1–4. www.aota.org/Publications-News/SISQuarterly/children-youth-practice-connections/SIPSIS-8-19.aspx.

Flaghouse. "Heavy Duty Tree Hanger." Accessed January 2, 2020. www.flaghouse.com/PE-New-2019/Heavy-Duty-Tree-Hanger.axd.

Fox, Kieran C. R., Savannah Nijeboer, Matthew L. Dixon, et al. "Is meditation associated with altered brain structure? A systematic review and meta-analysis of morphometric neuroimaging in meditation practitioners." *Neuroscience and Biobehavioral Reviews* 43 (June 2014): 48–73. doi.org/10.1016/j.neubiorev.2014.03.016.

Irlen. "What Is Irlen Syndrome?" The Irlen Institute. Accessed January 2, 2020. https://irlen.com/what-is-irlen-syndrome/.

Joyce, Andrew, Janet Etty-Leal, Tsharni Zazryn, and Amy Hamilton. "Exploring a Mindfulness Meditation Program on the Mental Health of Upper Primary Children: A Pilot Study." *Advances in School Mental Health Promotion* 3, no. 2 (April 2010): 17–25. doi.org/10.1080/1754730x.2010.9715677.

Kluge, Dr. Nicola. *Mindfulness for Kids: I: 7 Children's Meditations & Mindfulness Practices to Help Kids Be More Focused, Calm and Relaxed*. Houston, TX: Arts and Education Foundation, LLC, 2014.

Kuypers, Leah M., and Michelle Garcia Winner. *The Zones of Regulation: A Curriculum Designed to Foster Self-Regulation and Emotional Control*. Santa Clara, CA: Think Social Publishing, Inc., 2011.

Madrigal, Stephanie, and Michelle Garcia Winner. *Superflex: A Superhero Social Thinking Curriculum*. San Jose, CA: Think Social Publishing, Inc., 2008.

My Mundane and Miraculous Life (blog). "Occupational Therapy: Infinity Loop." February 2, 2016. Accessed January 2, 2020. www.mymundaneandmiraculouslife .com/occupational-therapy-infinity-loop/.

Napoli, Maria, Paul Rock Krech, and Lynn C. Holley. "Mindfulness Training for Elementary School Students." *Journal of Applied School Psychology* 21, no. 1 (June 2005): 99–125. doi.org/10.1300/j370v21n01_05.

Phillips, Hedy. "You Guys, the Science Behind Weighted Blankets Is Actually Fascinating." MSN.com. December 6, 2019. Accessed January 2, 2020. www .msn.com/en-us/health/wellness/you-guys-the-science-behind-weighted -blankets-is-actually-fascinating/ar-AAApGWa.

STAR Institute for Sensory Processing Disorder. "Subtypes of SPD." Accessed January 2, 2020. www.spdstar.org/basic/subtypes-of-spd.

STAR Institute for Sensory Processing Disorder. "Your 8 Senses." Accessed January 2, 2020. www.spdstar.org/basic/your-8-senses.

St. Lifer, Holly. "4 Common Types of Hearing Problems." AARP. Accessed January 2, 2020. www.aarp.org/health/conditions-treatments/info-04-2013/ common-hearing-problems.html.

Super Duper Publications. "Sensory Diet Cards." Accessed January 2, 2020. www.superduperinc.com/products/view.aspx?stid=554.

University of Minnesota. "How Does Mindfulness Work?" *Taking Charge of Your Health & Wellbeing.* Accessed January 2, 2020. www.takingcharge.csh.umn.edu/explore-healing-practices/mindfulness/how-does-mindfulness-work.

Williams, Mary Sue, and Sherry Shellenberger. *How Does Your Engine Run? A Leader's Guide to the Alert Program for Self-Regulation.* Albuquerque, NM: Therapy Works Inc., 1996.

Williams, Mary Sue, and Sherry Shellenberger. *Take Five!: Staying Alert at Home and School.* Albuquerque, NM: Therapy Works, Inc., 2001.

Williams, Mary Sue, and Sherry Shellenberger. *Test Drive: Introducing the Alert Program through Song.* Albuquerque, NM: Therapy Works, Inc., 2006.

Index

Acknowledgments

The saying "It takes a village" has never been more true. I'm sincerely grateful for all the inspiration and support received during this busy season of writing. Special thanks to:

Margaret Bledsoe, OTD, OTR/L, Isabel Polakof, MA, CCC-SLP, and Virginia Aguilar, MA for their professional dedication and review to make sure this book was accurate, comprehensive, and playful.

My friends, Victoria Barlow and Jamie Besel, for their thorough editing and reflections on what activities are actually meaningful and helpful.

My favorite toy-testers, helpful proofreaders, and technical consultants: my children Nicole, Victor, and Marie Foster.

My biggest fan and supporter, Jim Foster, for helping make this dream come true, especially when I need self-regulation.

My mother, Ellen Bavaro, who continues to support my self-regulation and goals with wisdom and resiliency.

Seth Schwartz and the team at Callisto Media for dedication to editing and publishing this much-needed resource.

The families of Kid's Work, who challenge me every day to listen and watch.

God, for giving me these gifts and faithfully allowing me to share my passion with others.

About the Author

Stephanie M. Foster, PhD, OTR/L, RYT, is an occupational therapist and proud mother of three sensational children. Her passion is helping children with a variety of special needs. Dr. Foster completed her BS in occupational therapy from Tufts University in 1988 and in pediatric occupational therapy from Boston University in 1994.

She received her PhD in prenatal and perinatal psychology from the Santa Barbara Graduate Institute in 2012.

Dr. Foster currently owns and operates Kid's Work, a small occupational therapy private practice dedicated to improving self-regulation through a non-pharmacological approach for families and children with sensory processing disorder. Her passion for self-regulation helps her create innovative therapies. She is known as a compassionate clinician, international lecturer, and author on the complexity of self-regulation and parenting.

She currently lives in Santa Maria, California, with her husband Jim, teenage daughter Marie, and Napoleon the therapy dog. For more information, visit KidsWork.biz.

Printed in the USA
CPSIA information can be obtained
at www.ICGtesting.com
CBHW040722210124
3521CB00001B/12